PAUL CATTERMOLE   SIMON FORTY

ARCHITECTS

FROM A TO Z

Prestel
Munich · London · New York

© Perrem & Cave Limited, 2013

Prestel Verlag, Munich
A member of Verlagsgruppe Random House GmbH

Prestel Verlag
Neumarkter Strasse 28
81673 Munich
Tel. +49 (0)89 4136-0
Fax +49 (0)89 4136-2335

Prestel Publishing Ltd.
4 Bloomsbury Place
London WC1A 2QA
Tel. +44 (0)20 7323-5004
Fax +44 (0)20 7636-8004

Prestel Publishing
900 Broadway, Suite 603
New York, NY 10003
Tel. +1 (212) 995-2720
Fax +1 (212) 995-2733

www.prestel.com

Library of Congress Control Number is available; British Library Cataloguing-in-
Publication Data: a catalogue record for this book is available from the British
Library; Deutsche Nationalbibliothek holds a record of this publication in the
Deutsche Nationalbibliografie; detailed bibliographical data can be found
under: www.dnb.de

Prestel books are available worldwide. Please contact your nearest bookseller
or one of the above addresses for information concerning your local distributor.

General Editor: Paul Cattermole
Project Coordination at Prestel: Stella Sämann
Design and layout: Suzanne Lemon
Production Director: Michelle Woo
Production at Prestel: René Fink

Full photo credits recorded on page 216
Entries by Paul Cattermole: PC
Entries by Simon Forty: SF

ISBN 978-3-7913-4773-8

Contents

"Every man builds his world in his own image."

The Fountainhead, 1943, Ayn Rand

Passionate, determined, daring: the hero of Ayn Rand's classic novel *The Fountainhead* personifies the popular image of the avant-garde architect as a troubled genius, straining to break the bounds of convention. Thrown out of his conservative college for his refusal to conform to traditional styles, Howard Roark embarks upon a tumultuous career dominated by his single-minded pursuit of a pure, modern architecture. Others seek to undermine him, usurp him or callously compromise his designs, but Roark remains devoted to his vision of what architecture can and should be.

Though modelled in part on the larger-than-life character of Frank Lloyd Wright, does Rand's fictional hero bear any relation to architecture as practised in the real world? Placing her emphasis on the single creative personality rather than the combined spread of professional expertise, Rand's perspective fails to convey the inherent complexities of creating buildings. Architecture is, by its very nature, a collective endeavour that requires the close cooperation of many minds and hands. Yet even in the modern world of multi-disciplinary design teams and armies of consultants, the idealized image of the architect as the ultimate creative voice endures. The popular perception of the architect's role remains that of 'fountainhead': the wellspring of ideas that creates a concept, then strives to preserve it at all costs.

By its very structure this book might appear to support this perception, focusing as it does on individuals by name, rather than teams by practice title. In that respect it is misleading, for though it casts its spotlight down a line of luminaries, each of its concise entries deliberately looks beyond the architect in question in search of the wider context of their work and the forces that brought it to fruition. These architects have been singled out amongst countless others for the way their collected works fit within the continuous evolution of their craft, creating a mirror in which we can view the society that commissioned them. In doing so they remind us that architecture does not exist in isolation, but is subject to the same external forces that shape every visual aspect of a culture: politics and faith, taste and technology, geography and history.

For these 200 individuals to have made their mark upon the world there had first to be the opportunity to build. As the eminent English architect Sir Edwin Lutyens once observed, 'There will never be great architects or great architecture without great patrons.' In many cases parents have provided the catalyst for great careers by giving young, untried architects the freedom to experiment in ways unthinkable within a conventional business relationship. Harry Seidler and Robert Venturi, to name but two, both benefitted from a mother's indulgence. In Seidler's case, a commission from his mother to build the first modernist house in Australia launched a career that would see him become that continent's leading exponent of the International Style. Venturi's work for his mother, on the other hand, was the first important essay in postmodernism and a textbook example of how architecture can be about more than simple functionality.

Having cut the apron strings, architects can further free themselves from clients' concerns by using their own homes as test beds for their ideas. The house that Charles and Ray Eames created for themselves in 1949 was in perfect synergy with the modern furniture they were designing at the time. Tailored to the Eameses' needs, their house remained relatively unchanged for decades and came to epitomize the informality of the new and modern Californian lifestyle. Frank Gehry, on the other hand, used the home he bought in Santa Monica in the 1970s as a design laboratory. It evolved as he constantly experimented with humble materials like corrugated metal and chain-link fence, finding ways to realize his deconstructed forms. For the architect willing to live within a building site, self-patronage can be the route to important new discoveries.

Affluent established architects can afford to turn their homes and studios into showrooms for their talents, inspiring their clients with confidence by effectively practising what they

The fraught evolution of the Solomon R. Guggenheim Museum, one of Frank Lloyd Wright's final works, illustrates why this architect's personality provided such rich source material for Ayn Rand's novel. Wright was invited to design the museum to house Guggenheim's collection of non-objective paintings in 1943, the same year The Fountainhead was published. The resulting 16-year struggle to bring the building into being was characterized by ongoing battles between the architect, the client, the local authorities and the art world over the appropriateness of the unconventional ziggurat design. In an uncompromising statement worthy of Howard Roark, Wright once waspishly declared that 'No details, (not even the smallest), can be interjected or interfered with without marring the peace and quiet of the whole Concept, Execution and Purpose.' Wright successfully defended the integrity of his inverted concrete spiral but sadly died six months before it was completed in 1959.

preach. Completed in 1898, Victor Horta's house in Brussels remains an outstanding example of the Art Nouveau style he helped to propagate. Filled with his signature whiplash tendrils, fluidly uniting the exposed structural elements, it offers a dynamic, organic interior that is a very personal expression of his design philosophy. Sir John Soane's London home is likewise a direct route to discovering the source of his design vocabulary. His neoclassical buildings derived much of their fine detail from his legendary collection of antiquaries, ranging from tiny seals to giant sarcophagi. Covering every available surface, this array of artefacts became as much a part of his interior design as the bold pigments on the walls and the ingenious coloured skylights with which he lit his compositions. Preserved today as living museums, the homes of Horta and Soane present two fine case studies of architects building their private worlds in their own image.

Lacking the budget to finance their own grand designs, many architects dream of a commission that gives them complete control over every element of the built environment, creating the opportunity for an immersive *Gesamtkunstwerk*: a total work of art. Often aspired to but rarely achieved, it requires a suitable site and budget, together with craftspeople and clients attuned to the architect's ideas. The results can be dramatic. John Nash's cacophony of chinoiserie at the Brighton Pavilion gave the flamboyant Prince Regent an oriental seaside whimsy that matched his decadent lifestyle. William Burges's labour of love, Cardiff Castle, likewise provided the 3rd Marquess of Bute with a medieval fantasy playground, far removed from the dirt and sweat of the family-owned coal port that financed it. Both dripped with ornate decoration and handmade details that sought to drown out the harsh realities of industrialization and

aid the retreat into a mythologized past. This is the architect building, not in his own image, but in the escapist mind-set of his patron. Burges was fortunate, for the Marquess of Bute's deep love of medievalism was one he shared, making this one of the most successful unions of architect and sponsor. Yet the pursuit of the *Gesamtkunstwerk* does not necessarily demand an abundance of decorative detail or the lavish application of colour and pattern. Creating a discrete harmony between every element of his scheme, Arne Jacobsen demonstrated a modernist vision for a total work of art at Oxford's St Catherine's College. In applying a consistent design rationale across every element, from the college halls to the canteen cutlery, Jacobsen was not trying to shut out the products of the modern world, but to refine and perfect them. The fact that his furniture designs remain in production to this day shows how adept Jacobsen was in paring back objects to their timeless essence.

Irrespective of the aesthetics, designing a building and its contents in their entirety takes time, talent and ultimately money, and the architect who single-mindedly pursues his or her artistic goals runs the risk of losing control altogether. A client's funds and patience are not infinite, and many architects have had to suffer the pain of being dismissed, then having to watch another complete their masterpiece. The prominence of the architect is no protection, for both John Vanbrugh's baroque explosion at Blenheim Palace and the sculptural shells of Jørn Utzon's Sydney Opera House were completed without them.

In addition to the constrictions of client and budget there is an even more fundamental matter governing whether architects can build a world in their own image: can their mental images be physically translated into three dimensions? In the age

Having bought a modest Dutch Colonial-style house in 1977, Frank Gehry shocked his Santa Monica neighbours the following year when he began to wreathe the original structure in successive layers of corrugated metal and eccentrically angled cubes of glazing. Deliberately using low-tech materials, Gehry was able to tinker with his domestic composition, expanding it in 1991 to accommodate his two growing teenaged sons. An icon for the Deconstructivist movement, its fragmented collection of parts gave Gehry many opportunities for exploring design avenues.

Sir John Soane also chose to remodel an existing building, slowly expanding across three adjoining terraced houses to create his eponymous museum. Like Gehry's home, Soane's was an accretion of his professional preoccupations, groaning under the scholarly weight of paintings and plaster casts that he accumulated over his prestigious career. Unable to expand further, he was obliged to devise a cunning means of hanging his art collection on hinged wall-sized panels that tripled the available surface area.

before architecture emerged as a defined profession, the medieval master masons of Europe were effectively designer, sculptor, surveyor and engineer, all rolled into one. Masters of their craft, they were able to realize great cathedrals, castles and palaces that still stand today, thanks to their holistic understanding of forces and materials gained through long apprenticeships and accumulated trade knowledge. Since the Renaissance, architecture has followed the pattern of wider society, with its practitioners becoming ever more focused upon a narrowing field of study. As the modernist architect Alvar Aalto once observed, 'Our time is so specialized that we have people who know more and more of less and less.' Along with this specialization, a desire for larger, taller and more complex structures has generated an increasing reliance on other professionals. Great engineering firms, such as those founded by Burro Happold, Peter Rice and Ove Arup, have become an indispensable part of the creative equation, to the point where the authorship of a building might be better credited jointly to architect and engineer. The modernist drive to reduce architecture to its essential structure effectively promoted the engineer's contribution, for now their work no longer lies hidden behind decorative facades of stone and brick. It was the skill with which the young Ove Arup engineered the Penguin Pool at London Zoo that permitted the poetry of Berthold Lubetkin's spiralling concrete ramps, and the story of twentieth-century architecture is filled with similar instances of buildings that owe their grace to the successful partnership of art and science.

Despite his quest to unite the visual arts under architecture, Bauhaus director Walter Gropius still felt there were boundaries between them and other professions, maintaining that

'architecture begins where engineering ends'. That divide is occasionally bridged when an architect combines more than one knowledge base, creating the opportunity for far greater self-expression. Antoni Gaudí's gothic brand of Art Nouveau derived its taut aesthetics from his appreciation of the forces transferring through his forests of organic vaults and columns. His greatest work, the Sagrada Família, was the product of detailed investigations into hyperbolic and catenary curves, which he saw expressed in nature. Gaudí's great innovation was to use gravity to help define his structures, suspending successive loops of cord or chain from inverted building plans, then weighting them with bags of lead shot to simulate the loads they would be required to carry. The tall, converging arches of his cathedral are the mirror image of these pioneering structural models, and a tangible example of how universal constants within engineering can still be interpreted into highly individual compositions.

Like Gaudí, fellow Catalan Santiago Calatrava gains greater freedom of expression by uniting architecture and engineering, having graduated with degrees in both professions. But whereas Gaudí's technical inspiration is partly obscured by his richly carved and inlaid decoration, Calatrava's modern route celebrates structural purity. The field in which he has had the greatest impact is in transport design, with stations that possess a sense of movement appropriate to their function, as well as expressing his recurring obsession with natural forms. His ability to assess both the aesthetics and structural viability of his own designs creates a more fluid and spontaneous exploration of ideas than would have been possible had he been reliant on outside expertise. Frank Gehry has similarly empowered himself, assuming control over his idiosyncratic forms by embracing

Though dealing with the same architectural junction of ceiling, wall and window, the deliberate aesthetics of Arne Jacobsen and Kendrick Kellogg could not be more dissimilar, and yet both are rare examples of a true Gesamtkunstwerk. With its reaching, tree-like roof supports sculpted by craftsman John Vugrin, Kellogg's High Desert House is a fluid piece of organic design where the furniture flows into the walls, like a dragon's tail snaking through the interior.

Despite sharing a broadly similar palette of concrete and glass, Jacobsen's dining hall for St Catherine's College is rigidly rectilinear, with its load-bearing columns set back from the walls so that their cantilevered ends float lightly in their haloes of glazing. Both designs seek to reduce the visual mass of their structures and focus attention on the quality of light that filters into the space.

advanced computer modelling programs. Having successfully experimented with the CATIA modelling packages borrowed from the aerospace industry, Gehry has invested heavily in this new technology, creating a whole new arm to his practice called Gehry Technologies. Using CATIA as its basis, the new 'Digital Project' software permits far greater precision in defining and costing building components, so that Gehry can work directly with contractors and manufacturers, convincing them that his complex forms are both affordable and buildable.

Clients, collaborators and technologies are only a few of the many external influences on architects, and yet the most radical changes to their work usually come from within. This A to Z of 200 architects contains many who dared to look hard at their existing body of work, then took the bold decision to set it aside and reach out for solutions as yet unknown. The ideological watershed of the early twentieth century provides many examples, thanks to the emergence of modernism and a host of other movements whose proponents made the conscious effort to break with the historicism of past styles. The advent of the Industrial Revolution created the demand for wholly new building types such as factories, railways stations and workers' housing, all with specific functional needs. These new design challenges combined with improvements in the mass production of cast iron, steel and glass were to provide the seeds of modernism. The architectural profession slowly began to divide, separating into those who sought to clothe the modern world in the trappings of past centuries, and the progressive generation who thought architecture should respond to the structural possibilities these new materials presented. This created an atmosphere of tense debate where radical exponents of

progress clashed with conservative practitioners unwilling to abandon tradition. Some early modernists deliberately set out to shock the old orders, advocating a stripping away of decoration and detail through both their work and words. In an uncompromising essay, Adolf Loos equated ornament to crime, while Le Corbusier's famously declared that 'the house is a machine for living in', both expressing a hard-line modernist desire to make a clean break with the past. Other designers were not so extreme, gradually effecting change through evolutionary means by refining their forms while still keeping contact with the past. The transitional works of Gunnar Asplund, Peter Behrens, Auguste Perret and Eliel Saarinen show why the first half of the twentieth century remains one of the most exciting architectural periods to study. Observing the development of their distinctive styles paints a vivid impression of a profession in a collective state of flux, from which would emerge the image of our modern world.

This shift away from historicism was not one-way traffic, however, and the advent of postmodernism after World War II saw many architects re-evaluate the central tenets of modernism, finding its unremitting functionalism wanting. The human desire for variety over uniformity began to reassert itself. Ironically it would be Le Corbusier, that high-priest of machined modernity, who would lead the way with his unique chapel at Ronchamp, whose seashell inspired roof form was the antithesis of his earlier rectilinear compositions. This dramatic sea change was something that many critics and fellow modernists found hard to accept, but the net result has been a far more pluralized definition of what constitutes a valid approach to architecture. Diversity in style makes for interesting monographs, but presents problems for illustrated A to Zs! Architects

Though still unrealized at the time of his death in 1926, Gaudí's Sagrada Família cathedral in Barcelona retains the spirit of his original design, which continues to govern its ongoing construction. Completed in 2000, the 45 m (150 ft)-tall nave remains true to Gaudí's 1:10 scale model. Its hyperbolic vault is supported by tree-like columns, which divide into splayed branches that radiate from egg-shaped capitals. Gaudí relied on physical models to resolve his design, but the current international team of architects and engineers have made extensive use of sophisticated modelling software so that the complex stone components can be economically machined instead of carved.

Calatrava's dual professional identity allows him to confidently sculpt his complex zoomorphic designs, which draw their inspiration from his studies of human anatomy. He has a particular fascination with skeletal structure and the batting eye, whose swooping brows and lashes are ideally suited to conveying a sense of movement. Completed in 1994, the flowing lines of the long platform concourse at the Lyon-Satolas TGV station combine elements of both. Resembling a prehistoric ribcage, its repetitive ranks of smooth concrete members were precisely cast in steel formwork to give that polished, bone-like finish.

such as Le Corbusier, Frank Lloyd Wright, Sir James Stirling and Sir Terry Farrell defy attempts to summarize their careers in a single image, precisely because their work explores so many avenues and aesthetics.

Along with this new plurality has come a renewed emphasis on the personal style of the individual architect, to the point where many have become international celebrities. Clients now come to their door with pre-conceived ideas of what will be delivered, wishing for instant icons in the mould of the architect's distinctive existing works. As creativity turns into a commodity, the progressive element of an architect's vision can become the first victim of their success. They begin to build in the image of their own image rather than respond to site or context. One of the greatest ironies of postmodern architecture in the era of the 'star-chitect' is that it risks repeating the uniformity of the international modernism that it supposedly rejects. Many of today's leading practitioners now design buildings so specific to their own style that they could be placed anywhere in the world, like imported pieces of sculpture. Celebrity can breed ubiquity at the expense of originality.

What does the future hold for the architectural profession? Does the advent of ever-more sophisticated software programs presage an age of the all-powerful architect, one who exerts complete control over his or her creations like a master mason of old? Will the talent and creativity of key individuals increasingly dominate the design process? Certainly the name above the practice door retains its potency, frequently becoming a brand that ambitious clients can buy into, as though it was a fashion label. Headline-grabbing 'star-chitects' such as Baron Norman Foster, Frank Gehry, Rem Koolhaas and Dame Zaha Hadid now attract commissions from around the globe simply by virtue of their high-profile status. It is as though cities have become collectors, seeking to complete their own architectural A to Zs. Ayn Rand's words now seem prophetic, for the architectural elite appears to be populating the world in the image of its own work.

Though the big name practices continue to dominate the commissions for art galleries and skyscrapers, they remain the tip of the architectural iceberg. Away from the glare of the public eye, the bulk of the wider profession presses on with designing the fabric of our day-to-day world: hospitals and housing, surgeries and schools, shops and swimming pools, restaurants and leisure centres. Though often working to demanding briefs with finite resources, lesser-known architects still manage to fight and win small design victories, slowly improving the net quality of our built environment, one commission at a time. They benefit from the trickle-down effect as large practices with money to invest develop the customized software that further reduces the labour involved in modelling and testing designs. With powerful digital tools at their disposal, small practices can begin to compete on ever-bigger stages, and carve out great careers from modest beginnings.

One page is a narrow window through which to view a life spent in architecture but these 200 entries still offer tantalizing insights into the heads that guide the hands. Once you have glanced through that window, we hope you will be encouraged to open the door and discover more about these men and women who have helped shape the image of our world.

Paul Cattermole, 2012

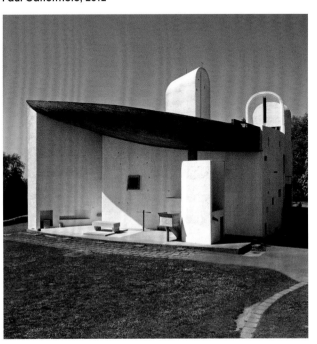

No record of twentieth-century architecture can be considered complete without mention of Le Corbusier and two of his most iconic projects. Raised above its broad expanse of green lawn upon slender round piloti, the Villa Savoye was a veritable manifesto for modernist architecture when it was completed in 1931, combining all of the 'Five Points' that Le Corbusier had outlined in his Vers une architecture eight years earlier. With an open-plan layout and reinforced concrete construction, its promise of an efficient 'machine for living in' was dented only by defects in workmanship, which led to recurring problems with a leaking roof.

Le Corbusier continued to design in this highly rational manner for the next 20 years, proposing entire cities ordered along similar modernist lines. It therefore came as a great shock to many of his ardent supporters when this piloti of the modernist establishment unveiled his chapel of Notre Dame du Haut at Ronchamp in 1954. The contrast could not be more marked. The white exterior remained, but instead of continuous strip windows, a seemingly random composition of deep niches filled with coloured glass were punched into its thick walls. The building was now firmly anchored to the ground, while the free-form curves of the coarse cast-concrete roof floated just above the walls on tiny columns to create a halo of light. Highly original and influential, it remains one of the boldest public U-turns in architectural history.

Aalto Alvar

Riola Parish Church | Church of the Assumption of Mary

Dates: 1898–1976 **Nationality:** Finnish **Location:** Riola di Verga (near Bologna), Italy **Date Completed:** 1978 **Style | Movement:** Modernist

The work of Alvar Aalto is iconic, influential and remarkably consistent, from the small scale of a rippling glass vase or supple wooden chair up to a national concert hall. Aalto began as a practitioner of a refined Nordic Classicism but later became a leading light in the development of modernism. After winning the competition for the Paimio Sanatorium in 1929, he detailed every aspect of it down to the door handles, in his quest to meet the patients' needs for rest and sunlight. His later structures are more organic and asymmetrical, exemplifying a humane and fluid approach to functionality. Rooted in nature and his homeland, they were inspired by simple sinuous wave forms and the slender clustered trunks of Finland's pine forests. One of Aalto's final works, completed two years after his death, was this modest parish church in the north of Italy, where a succession of decreasing pre-cast concrete arches echoes the laminated frames of the famous plywood chairs he had designed for the sanatorium nearly 50 years earlier. They swoop over the worshippers and support a gently curving roof, whose staggered, glazed scopes once again ensure that peace and light are a central part of a carefully considered human experience. **PC**

Adam Robert

Dates: 1728–92 **Nationality:** Scottish **Location:** Isleworth, Middlesex, England **Date Completed:** 1769 **Style|Movement:** Neoclassical

In the Age of Enlightenment, no young gentleman's education was considered complete until he had undertaken the Grand Tour of Europe. While many members of the aristocracy merely brought back souvenirs, this son of a Scottish architect returned with a body of work that was to reshape a nation's taste. Robert Adam spent four years diligently studying the ruins of France and Italy, then used the catalogues of motifs and details he had compiled to forge a style all his own. 'Adamesque' decoration was free of the strict rules of Palladian Classicism, happily combining Roman, Greek and Etruscan elements into light and airy schemes of unified ornamentation that could be consistently applied across ceilings, walls, floors and furniture. Backed by an entourage of skilled craftsmen and artificers, Adam became the master of applied design, and within two years of his return to England in 1758 he was commissioned by the 1st Duke of Northumberland to remodel his rooms at Syon Park. Adam distilled his studies of Roman basilicas into the imperial splendour of the Great Hall, which is packed with classical motifs from coffered niches to delicate plaster friezes, picked out in cool, pale tones. It remains a suitably impressive start for a grand tour of the Duke's home. **PC**

Alberti Leon Battista

Dates: 1404–72 **Nationality:** Italian (born Genoa) **Location:** Florence, Italy **Date Completed:** 1470 **Style | Movement:** Renaissance

From any perspective, Leon Battista Alberti was the perfect Renaissance man. Handsome and witty, an adept mathematician and artist, he rose from inauspicious beginnings—he was the illegitimate son of Lorenzo Alberti, whose politicking saw him driven out of Florence and into exile—to become the friend of popes and the embodiment of the humanist architect. On the way he collaborated with Paolo Toscanelli (who would supply Columbus with maps for his first voyage) and wrote a treatise on perspective—*De Pictura*, dedicated to Brunelleschi, who had inspired him—as well as the first book on cryptography, containing the first example of a frequency table, and the first Renaissance treatise on architecture, *De re aedificatoria*. Published in 1485, it leant heavily on Vitruvius and educated succeeding generations of architects on the harmonious relationship between science and art. The facade of the Basilica of Santa Maria Novella—the first of Florence's great basilicas—provides a perfect example of his ideas, marrying geometric figures with classical features in a striking harmony. The work was financed by Alberti's patron, the Florentine merchant Giovanni di Paolo Rucellai, whose name adorns the pediment and whose family crest, in the form of a row of ships, can be seen on the cornice. **SF**

Dates: 1512–72 **Nationality:** Italian (born Perugia, Papal States) **Location:** Milan, Italy **Date Completed:** 1567 **Style|Movement:** Mannerist

Vasari thought him 'a talented and most excellent architect'; Michelangelo was his friend in Rome; Phillip II sent for him to work in Spain—but it is for his work in Genoa and Milan that Alessi is best remembered. Born in Perugia, he studied under painter and architect Giovanni Battista Caporali and showed early enthusiasm for the architecture of antiquity. He spent some years in Genoa, where he was involved in the planning of the Strada Nuova in the 1550s—today known as Via Garibaldi and a World Heritage Site—ensuring that the sumptuous palaces lining the street achieved an overall harmony and contributed to Genoa's nickname—la *Superba*. In Milan he designed the Palazzo Marino (completed 1561), now the City Hall, whose facade and internal court are fine examples of Mannerist decoration. His renovation and expansion of the Church of St Barnabas and St Paul remodelled the original church along counter-reformation lines, in accord with the attempts of the Catholic Church to reach out to its divided congregation: a substantial nave, which ensured all could see the altar and hear the sermon, was separated from the choir by a transverse presbytery. The lower facade has lost its stucco embellishments but the interior is notable for Corinthian columns in the nave that act as entrances for side chapels. **SF**

Dates: Born 1947   **Nationality:** English   **Location:** London, England   **Date Completed:** 2000   **Style | Movement:** Postmodernist

A flamboyant character and eloquent orator who considers himself as much artist as architect, Will Alsop has long enjoyed his reputation as the *enfant terrible* of British architecture. His buildings are as singular as the mind behind them, and not without their detractors, but few could deny their playful energy. In 2000, the prestigious Stirling Prize was awarded to Alsop and his then-partner Jan Störmer for their witty and worthy Peckham Library with its daring form, vibrant colour palette and organic learning 'pods'. An inverted copper-clad capital 'L', cantilevering out on a tangle of impossibly spindly 'legs', the design cleverly raises the reading rooms above the street noise, creating a covered public space in the process. The silhouette culminates with bold signage and a jaunty red beret roof capping a raised halo of windows that flood the interior with natural light. The rear facade is clad in bold stained-glass panels that hint at Alsop's admiration for the concentrated colour of Sir John Soane and Le Corbusier. Peckham remains one of London's toughest boroughs but Alsop succeeded in making a place of learning an inviting environment where the whole community felt welcome. **PC**

Andō Tadao

Dates: Born 1941 **Nationality:** Japanese **Location:** Tokyo, Japan **Date Completed:** 1986 **Style | Movement:** Minimalist

Despite no formal training, Tadao Andō has achieved a revered position within modern architecture. He is known for perfect compositions, minimally detailed so that their occupants may focus on the purity of the proportions and the subtle play of light. His use of plain concrete surfaces can give his domestic buildings a monastic look, but when experienced first-hand, they are spiritual rather than severe. Andō's ability to create a sense of calm internal order is beautifully demonstrated in his Kidosaki House, where he surrounded the suburban plot with tall concrete curtain walls, then placed a large 'keep' at its centre before subdividing the composition into a grid of squares. The only curved components are the sweeping entrance wall and stair, which allow space for off-street parking. Privacy was a concern, as the large home was to be shared by three families: a couple and both their respective parents. Andō succeeded in interlocking rooms of varying heights to discretely quarter the three couples, while leaving light-filled shared communal areas like the courtyard, where the family could reunite. A concrete reinterpretation of Japanese vernacular architecture, Andō's work has consistently employed the same family of forms and finishes to ethereal effect. **PC**

Andreu Paul

Dates: Born 1938   **Nationality:** French   **Location:** Beijing, China   **Date Completed:** 2007   **Style|Movement:** High Tech

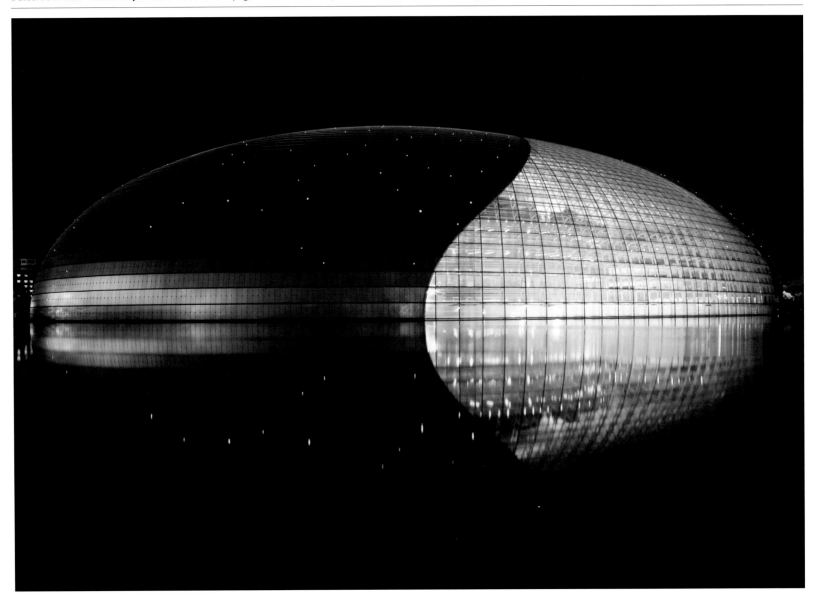

Having studied both architecture and engineering, Andreu became a go-to man for airports, starting on home ground with all three Paris airports: Orly, Le Bourget and Charles de Gaulle. Undaunted by size, he has accepted large-scale commissions from some of the biggest clients in the world, and he has built airports in Manila, Jakarta, Shanghai, Abu Dhabi, Dubai, Cairo and Brunei. Andreu is best known in his home country for the monumental

Grande Arche at La Défense, having taken over the architectural responsibility for its construction from its original designer, Johann Otto von Spreckelsen—the endpoint of a triumphal way that starts at the Louvre and passes through the Arc du Carrousel and the Arc de Triomphe. Built for the 2008 Olympic Games, Beijing's National Centre for the Performing Arts, known affectionately as the Bird's Egg (to accompany the Bird's Nest Stadium) is a futuristic ellipsoid

titanium and glass dome surrounded by an artificial lake. Entered by a hall under the lake, it houses the opera, music and theatre halls with a combined capacity of nearly 5,500. In this and his other works, Andreu uses his global experience to design clean solutions for modern society, exploiting the latest architectural technologies to make structures that are unfussy and seamlessly functional. **SF**

Arad Ron

Dates: Born 1951   **Nationality:** Israeli   **Location:** Tel Aviv, Israel   **Date Completed:** 2010   **Style | Movement:** Contemporary Modern

Though he trained as an architect, Ron Arad has spent much of his career working at a smaller scale, producing furniture as well as numerous product designs. His style evolved from industrial ready-mades, using old Rover car seats and scaffolding poles, to highly sculptural handmade pieces such his 1986 'Well Tempered Chair' for Vitra, composed solely of looped sheets of steel bolted together in self-sprung hoops. His 12 years as the head of the Department of Design Products at London's Royal College of Art made him an international figure in design circles and his commission to give form to a design museum for Tel Aviv united all his skills and knowledge. Two rectangular concrete volumes are linked by an oval entrance hall; all three elements are swaddled in soaring ribbons of colourful Corten steel, which bind them together and create a sheltered courtyard in their midst. The fluidity of this piece of space-defining sculpture contrasts with the restraint of the simple top-lit gallery spaces; Arad's own exhibition design experience makes him conscious that the architecture should not attempt to upstage the exhibits. A triumphant return to the discipline he left some 30 years before, this museum has proven he is still in the loop. **PC**

Asplund Gunnar Erik

Dates: 1885–1940 **Nationality:** Swedish **Location:** Stockholm, Sweden **Date Completed:** 1928 (Fourth wing added in 1932) **Style | Movement:** Nordic Neoclassical

The most influential of Swedish architects, Gunnar Asplund was one of a select generation who mark the transition from historical styles to true modernism. His work helped define Nordic Classicism, but was gradually refined until pure, abstract geometry became his focus. His Stockholm Public Library displays these modernist inclinations. The central element is the immensely high drum tower, tightly flanked on each side by four rectangular wings from which it appears to rise. The drum is lined by three floors of bookcases, accessed by continuous balconies that hug the walls. Originally envisaging a grand glazed dome above its central reading room, Asplund made the bold decision to cap it with an understated flat roof and insert a halo of unadorned square windows to bring in natural light. The symmetrical plan is a model of functional clarity, with clear entry axes and circulation routes that create a natural flow of readers around the space. The bold rust-red rendered facades are set with elegant pale stone frames and modest mouldings: the last trace of neoclassical detail on what is essentially a rationalized modern structure. The library was a place of learning within Asplund's own development, just as it continues to be for the readers who use it. **PC**

Dates: 1865–1945   **Nationality:** Scottish   **Location:** Lake District, England   **Date Completed:** 1900   **Style | Movement:** Arts and Crafts

After training with the City Architect of Bath, Mackay Baillie Scott moved to the Isle of Man in 1889. His early ornate medieval style soon evolved into a more simplified approach that celebrated precise craftsmanship, emphasizing materials and function—a mantra that influenced, most notably, Frank Lloyd Wright. Baillie Scott was also a serious furniture designer, working closely with John P. White of Bedford. The important thing, he said, was to ensure that each piece had an 'exquisite appropriateness to its position and to its use'. He worked on a range of large, comfortable domestic buildings—some 300 in his lifetime—and prospered in an age of wealthy, cultured patronage, when rich men liked to build their own distinctive homes. Blackwell, near Lake Windermere—a short distance from Ruskin's house on Coniston Water—was built as a holiday home for Sir Edward Holt, a wealthy Manchester brewer. It is a wonderful mix of heavy, half-timbered and panelled work—as in the huge central hall (shown here) —and light-filled rooms exemplified by the luminous White Drawing Room. The detailing is typically Arts and Crafts, from the ornate decoration on the drainpipes to the stained glass in the dining room. **SF**

Barragán Luis

Dates: 1902–88   **Nationality:** Mexican   **Location:** Fraccionamiento los Cubes, Mexico   **Date Completed:** 1968   **Style|Movement:** Regional Modernist

While some ideas get lost in translation, others grow richer. After graduating in 1923 as an engineer, Luis Barragán left his native Mexico to travel in Europe and explore the Moorish architecture of Morocco and Spain. The tranquil gardens of the Alhambra, with tinkling pools and channels, left an indelible mark on his imagination, as did lectures by Le Corbusier that he attended during a subsequent trip to Paris in 1931. Barragán had already begun practising as an architect in 1926, and he steadily evolved a unique and highly personal synthesis of modernism and Mexican vernacular. His simple palette of humble materials was luminously brought to life with vertical planes of pure colour, standing bright and bold like abstract paintings in an outdoor gallery. At San Cristóbal the bulk of the long, low stable block lies hidden behind a simple roughcast wall, which upon closer inspection reveals itself to be largely hollow, hiding an aqueduct between its faces. The water cascades from a short spout at the channel's end to fill the large pool, deep enough for hot horses to wade waist deep after a long ride. Today, Barragán's influence can be found not only in architecture but also translated into many contemporary garden designs. **PC**

Barry Charles

Dates: 1795–1860 **Nationality:** English **Location:** London, England **Date Completed:** 1852, House of Commons; 1874, House of Lords **Style | Movement:** Gothic Revival

The Victorian era in Britain was a time of great expansion and wealth, as well as an increasing tendency in public taste for classically monumental buildings. One of the greatest Victorian architects of all was born in Bridge Street, Westminster, within sight of the site of what would be his greatest architectural triumph. Charles Barry cut his teeth designing Italianate churches for the Church of England Commissioners after doing the Grand Tour around Italy between 1817 and 1820. He returned to England a confirmed fan of Renaissance architecture, an influence he made evident in all his buildings, using the Florentine palazzo style in works such as the Travellers Club in Pall Mall, London (1829). When the old Palace of Westminster was consumed by fire in 1834, Barry won the public competition to design a new home for Parliament. He produced a Renaissance-inspired building overlaid with gothic detailing; the latter provided by his architectural collaborator Augustus Pugin. Some parts of the medieval palace survived the flames and were skilfully incorporated into the new building. Barry was knighted for his work in 1852. Three of Barry's sons became architects, with Edward finishing his father's work on the Palace of Westminster. **SF**

Bawa Geoffrey

Sri Lankan Parliament Complex

Dates: 1919–2003   **Nationality:** Sri Lankan   **Location:** Diyawanna Oya, Kotte, Sri Lanka   **Date Completed:** 1985   **Style | Movement:** Regional Modernist

Geoffrey Bawa took time to find his true place and profession in life. Born in what was then Ceylon, but educated in England, he came close to settling in Italy but instead returned home in 1948 and bought land, with the intention of building a house and garden there. Realizing he lacked the necessary knowledge, he retrained as an architect, qualifying at the age of 38. Bawa's passion for Sri Lanka's heritage led him to evolve a geo-specific style that reinterpreted essential elements of the local vernacular. Sri Lanka's new parliament exemplifies his consistent striving to fuse history with modernity. The site had special significance as the former location of a palace built by the powerful fourteenth-century minister, Nissaka Alakesvara. Bawa suggested the swampy ground be dredged to form an artificial lake, in which the copper-roofed complex now sits serenely on its island, like a pre-colonial waterside palace. Beneath the sweeping lines of the high pitched roofs, Bawa arranged a careful marriage of indigenous details with a modern plan, using concrete, stone and timber in layered storeys of ever-finer pillars and screens. It is to Sri Lanka's benefit that Bawa made that decision to come home. **PC**

Behrens Peter

Dates: 1868–1940 **Nationality:** German **Location:** Berlin, Germany **Date Completed:** 1909 **Style|Movement:** Early Modernist

When Peter Behrens designed his first piece of architecture in 1899, he set out to create a *Gesamtkunstwerk:* a total work of art. His Behrens Haus, completed in 1901, was filled with handmade objects that he had designed in a romantic style, which owed much to the prevailing British Arts and Crafts and German *Jugendstil* movements. Ironically, thanks to his subsequent close association with the German General Electrical Company, AEG,

Behrens would go on to be celebrated as a pioneer of industrial design for mass production. Engaged in 1907 as their artistic director, he became the first designer in history to have total control over a company's corporate identity, responsible for not only the products themselves, but the logo stamped upon them, the posters that promoted them and the building where some of them were made. With its austere but imposing concrete facade, inspired by

Ancient Egyptian pylons, the AEG Turbine Factory is a veritable temple to industry, with the company logo incised like a Pharaonic cartouche. Behrens purposefully expressed the supporting steel frame structure, spanned by tall glass windows down each side. Filled with light and with objects of his design, Behrens had this time created a *Gesamtkunstwerk* on an industrial scale. **PC**

Dates: 1856–1934   **Nationality:** Dutch   **Location:** Amsterdam, Netherlands   **Date Completed:** 1903   **Style | Movement:** Modernist

Dubbed the 'Father of Modern Architecture' in the Netherlands, Hendrik Berlage is known for his ideas for architectural purity, presented through bold designs, and is credited with bridging the void between the European traditionalists and modernists. He studied in Zurich in the 1870s, spent some time travelling through Europe, and afterwards went into partnership with Theodore Sanders in Holland. After visiting the United States he came home heavily influenced by the employment of building materials for their fundamental properties; in particular, he was impressed by the wood-based, organic architecture of Louis Sullivan and Frank Lloyd Wright and the elegant Neo-Romanesque brickwork detailing of Henry Hobson Richardson. Berlage incorporated these ideas into his trademark building, the Beurs van Berlage, the (now former) Amsterdam Commodities Exchange, a modernist collection of three trading halls, offices and public spaces, in red brick, iron and glass, featuring Romanesque arches and finished off with an asymmetric clock tower. Largely devoid of decoration, the building has a series of tableaux by Jan Toorop inside the main entrance. The ground-breaking central hall is a vast, glass-covered space supported by unadorned steel arches. It introduced the idea of a radically new architecture to Europe and heavily influenced the subsequent Amsterdam School. **SF**

Bernini Gian Lorenzo

Colonnades in front of St. Peter's Basilica

Dates: 1598–1680   **Nationality:** Italian (born Naples)   **Location:** Rome, Italy   **Date Completed:** 1667   **Style | Movement:** Baroque

Perhaps best known for his Fountain of the Four Rivers in Rome's Piazza Navona, Bernini created eye-catching work: he knew how to draw attention to a subject with highly elaborate design and the intelligent use of light and optical effects. Through his absolute mastery of his profession he was unquestionably the supreme artist of the Baroque style. A Neapolitan by birth, Bernini made his name in Rome. He learnt to sculpt marble in his father's studio and received his first formal commission from Cardinal Scipione Borghese, for a series of larger-than-life statues for his Roman villa. His incomparable skill with marble, especially with works such as *The Ecstasy of St Teresa* (1652), earned him a summons from the *Roi Soleil* himself to work on the Louvre Palace. However, he was also a significant architect. He contributed magnificent features to St Peter's for Popes Urban VIII and Alexander VII, who commissioned his final work for the Holy See: a design for the grand piazza in front of St Peter's Basilica, for which Bernini devised a huge oval space defined by two freestanding colonnades that he described as the welcoming arms of the mother church embracing her children. Today one cannot imagine St Peter's without it. **SF**

Blom Piet

Dates: 1934–99 **Nationality:** Dutch **Location:** Rotterdam, Netherlands **Date Completed:** 1984 **Style|Movement:** Structuralist

Many architects find inspiration in natural structures but few translate them as literally as Piet Blom. Initially trained as a carpenter, Blom enrolled at the Academy of Architecture in Amsterdam and became a pupil of Aldo van Eyck. Van Eyck and his circle were strongly influenced by the French anthropologist, Claude Lévi-Strauss, whose theory of Structuralism maintained that the structure of society is derived from its under-lying network of relationships. For van Eyck, translating these ideas

from anthropology to architecture meant letting these social structures guide the design of his buildings, rather than allowing technology to take the lead. Inspired by this idea, Blom focused on creating collective village-like buildings, which he described as 'living under an urban roof'. His Rotterdam Kubuswoningen (Cubic Houses) present a continuous abstract forest canopy whose 38 tree-like dwellings adopt the form of interlocking cubes, each balanced on its corner on brick and

concrete 'trunks'. The four upper faces are roof and wall in one, with sharply inclined planes anchored directly to its concrete floor plates. In this abstract, geometric grove each 'tree' touches its neighbour to provide mutual support—perhaps a metaphor for Blom's desire to foster social interaction. In continuous occupation since their completion, Blom's arboreal urban community certainly convinced humans to return to the trees once more. **PC**

Böhm Gottfried

Dates: Born 1920   **Nationality:** German   **Location:** Potsdam, Germany   **Date Completed:** 2006   **Style|Movement:** Contemporary Modern

When Gottfried Böhm first approaches a project, he begins by considering how to make it sit harmoniously within its setting without looking incongruous: what form it should take, what size and shape, which materials this requires and what colours the building should have. Böhm likes to think of himself as a creator who connects the past to the future and the building to the environment as well as a catalyst who can turn the magic of a creative idea into physical reality. The results of this approach are lyrical, otherworldly buildings of often extraordinary design: part science fiction, part castles of the imagination. Over his long career he has designed everything from homes to offices, cultural centres and civic centres, museums, theatres and churches. The five-storey Hans-Otto-Theatre in Potsdam pays homage to Jørn Utzon's Sydney Opera House, with a concrete structure, huge walls of glass and a series of cantilevered wings, all overlooking the Tiefer See. Böhm's work is hard to categorize: some consider him to be keeping Expressionism alive, while others prefer the term post-Bauhaus. Whichever applies, he is unfailingly unconventional. He still runs the family architectural practice he inherited from his father from its offices in Cologne. **SF**

Borromini Francesco

San Carlo alle Quattro Fontane

Dates: 1599–1667   **Nationality:** Italian (born Bissone, Ticino, Swiss confederacy)   **Location:** Rome, Italy   **Date Completed:** 1641 (Consecrated 1646)   **Style | Movement:** Baroque

The tragic drama of Francesco Borromini began in 1619, when the talented young stonemason moved to Rome to work on St Peter's, first under Carlo Maderno then under his successor, Gian Lorenzo Bernini. Only a year apart in age, the two men could not have been more different. Borromini was melancholic and quick tempered, while Bernini was suave and polished, attracting the commissions and acclaim that Borromini thought should be his.

Frustrated at being the subordinate, Borromini left St Peter's, resolving to outdo his bitter rival. His debut solo commission was the breathtaking San Carlo alle Quattro Fontane: a small church on the Quirinal Hill that forms part of a complex of monastic buildings. Cunningly inserted into an awkward corner site, it remains one of the most spatially inventive interiors ever composed, the intensity of its geometric plotting only being revealed in plan. With the feet of its

supporting arches partially concealed by projecting mouldings, the oval dome appears to hover high above the worshippers' heads, its deeply coffered patterns of octagons, crosses and hexagons thrown into high relief by natural light. Yet, despite such theatrical successes, Borromini remained a troubled soul, and in his final act, he took his own life with a sword. **PC**

28

Botta Mario

Dates: Born 1943 **Nationality:** Swiss **Location:** Mogna, Ticino, Switzerland **Date Completed:** 1998 **Style|Movement:** Modernist

Mario Botta's work possesses a natural gravitas, born of brick and stone construction, which is particularly appropriate for religious architecture. Botta began designing buildings aged just 16, evolving a vocabulary of pure solids that he carves and slices with consummate skill. Botta prefers materials formed over thousands of years, with a richness that helps relieve the simplicity of his forms. Much of his work is in his native Ticino, an Italian-speaking Swiss canton with steep alpine terrain, and in 1986, when a landslide obliterated the seventeenth-century church in Mogno, Botta was commissioned to replace it. The striking elliptic cylinder of his church is composed of alternating layers of Peccia marble and Vallemaggia granite, both sourced from local quarries. Facing up the slope, like a buttress braced against the forces of nature, the striped cylinder is sliced off at an angle so that the glass roof is perfectly circular. The only source of natural light, this roof is divided by two flying arches supporting chevrons of glazing bars that cast a second layer of stripes across the walls. The landslide may have swept all away before it, but Botta's considered mass of masonry ensures a lasting legacy, rooted in the local landscape. **PC**

Dates: 1694–1753   **Nationality:** English   **Location:** London, England   **Date Completed:** 1729   **Style | Movement:** Neo-Palladian

Although a privy councillor and member of the House of Lords, Richard Boyle, 3rd Earl of Burlington, was much more interested in arts and culture. He made three Grand Tours, during which time he fell in love with Andrea Palladio's work, taking copious architectural notes as he toured the Veneto in 1719. On his return he decided to change the designs of the Baroque architect working on Burlington House in Piccadilly. In collaboration with new architect James Gibbs, Boyle took over the design himself. The result was a neo-Palladian building with William Kent interiors. In 1725, Boyle's family summer home, beside the Thames in southwest London, burnt down. He seized the opportunity to redesign Chiswick House in Palladian style with an Italianate landscape garden by Kent. Heavily inspired by Palladio's Villa Rotunda in Vicenza, Chiswick House was designed as a space to entertain guests and to contain the art and furniture he had collected during his travels. It had no bedrooms and no kitchen. The house was surmounted by a coffered dome modelled on the Basilica of Maxentius and Constantine, in the Forum at Rome. The villa was such a critical success that by the 1730s the Palladian style was the fashionable look for every new grand house across the land and Horace Walpole dubbed Boyle the 'Apollo of the Arts'. **SF**

Bramante Donato

Dates: 1444–1514   **Nationality:** Italian (born Fermignano, Urbino)   **Location:** Rome, Italy   **Date Completed:** 1502   **Style | Movement:** Renaissance

Donato Bramante began his training as an apprentice to two great Renaissance artists—first, Mantegna and then Piero della Francesca—but he soon turned to architecture. His first important patron was Ludovico Sforza, Duke of Milan. He he worked in Milan for some 25 years before moving to Rome. There he found patronage from Cardinal Della Rovere who later became Pope Julius II. Bramante worked in the grand manner, a style particularly suited to the swaggering opulence of buildings around the Vatican. He put his early artistic training to good use by playing with perspective and incorporating illusionistic features into his buildings. He designed his architectural masterpiece, the Tempietto in the cloister of San Pietro in Montorio on the Janiculum, on the site where St Peter was thought to have been crucified. Domed and colonnaded, this jewel of a building was loosely modelled on the ancient Theatre of Marcellus. The circular plan symbolizes divine perfection. It was designed to be seen from the outside—the inside space is only 5 m (15 ft) in diameter— and Bramante wanted to add a courtyard but Julius wanted him to revamp St Peter's instead. Few of Bramante's buildings have survived intact: most have been considerably altered over the centuries. Consequently, Bramante's principal legacy is the inspiration he provided to his successors. **SF**

Brunelleschi Filippo

The Basilica di Santa Maria del Fiore | Duomo

Dates: 1377–1446   **Nationality:** Florentine   **Location:** Florence, Italy   **Date Completed:** Consecrated 1436; lantern finished 1461; facade completed 1887   **Style | Movement:** Renaissance

Filippo Brunelleschi was a true Renaissance man and the first modern engineer. He apprenticed as a sculptor and goldsmith but was more interested in mechanics and engineering and, in particular, mathematics and geometry. His studies led him to rediscover the principles of linear perspective using mirrors and the importance of the vanishing point. In the early fifteenth century, the prevailing architectural headache in Florence was how to complete Santa Maria del Fiore—*fiore* (flower) refers to the lily, the symbol of Florence. A competition was announced in 1418 to solve the problem, the core of which was how to place a circular dome on top of the existing octagonal baptistery. Putting his geometry and mathematical skills to use, Brunelleschi proposed a double self-supporting shell and rib framework to carry the enormous weight of the more than four million bricks that would make up the dome in a rotating herring-bone pattern. The bracing would be provided by a huge lantern above the centre of the dome. He also devised a system of counter-weights and lifts with the world's first reverse gear to obviate the need for wooden scaffolding. His submission was accepted and the stunning dome was complete and awaiting the final touches of lantern, gilt copper ball and cross when Brunelleschi died in 1446. **SF**

Buonarroti Michelangelo

Dates: 1475–1564 **Nationality:** Italian (born Caprese, Tuscany) **Location:** Rome, Italy **Date Completed:** c.1650 **Style | Movement:** Renaissance

Rome's ancient Capitoline Hill—today's Campidoglio—was the political and religious heart of Rome for more than 2,500 years. However, by the sixteenth century it had deteriorated, and in 1536 Pope Paul III decided to redevelop the area in preparation for a visit from Holy Roman Emperor Charles V. He turned to Italy's greatest living artist to design the new work: Michelangelo, who had a well-established reputation as a sculptor, painter and poet. Typically, Michelangelo produced a plan to reconstruct the entire area on an epic scale. He redesigned the Palazzo Senatorio (the Roman senate), provided a new facade for the thirteenth-century Palazzo dei Conservatori and designed a new building opposite it, the Palazzo Nuovo. For the Piazza del Campidoglio itself he designed an intriguing geometric ground pattern, in the centre of which he placed the ancient equestrian statue of Marcus Aurelius. To bring pedestrians up to the piazza from the Piazza d'Aracoeli at the bottom of the hill, he proposed the Cordonata, a monumental staircase wide enough for horsemen to ascend without dismounting. Work had barely started when the emperor arrived in 1538, and had not progressed very far when Michelangelo himself died. Indeed, the scheme was not completed until the seventeenth century and the paving design until 1940—but today most of the Piazza del Campidoglio is as Michelangelo envisaged it. **SF**

Burges William

Dates: 1827–81   **Nationality:** English   **Location:** Cardiff, Wales   **Date Completed:** 1881   **Style|Movement:** Arts and Crafts / Gothic Revival

William Burges was one of the most important architect/designers of the Arts and Crafts movement and a leader of the Gothic Revival. His own personal interests and areas of knowledge included medieval metalwork and gothic arts and antiquities in general. Unsurprisingly, his decorative tastes found great accord with ecclesiastical institutions and he designed many churches and even cathedrals. He incorporated gothic detailing into his own works, often expressing a distinct sense of humour along the way. One of his most important commissions came in 1865 from the 3rd Marquess of Bute (at that point, one of the richest men in the world) to refurbish his family home, Cardiff Castle, whose history dates back to Roman times. This massive job included the building of a new library; erection of the Bute, Clock, Herbert, Guest and Tank Towers; restoration of the fifteenth-century Octagon Tower; and a new banqueting hall on the site of the old medieval hall. The marquess was also a Gothic Revival enthusiast and allowed his extravagant architect considerable latitude. In return, he gained, both inside and out, a fairy-tale medieval castle. Burges's work was cut short when he died in 1881 but his erstwhile assistant, William Frame, continued working on the castle and on another of Burges's remarkable creations for the marquess: Castell Coch above Tongwynlais village north of Cardiff. **SF**

Burnham Daniel Hudson

Dates: 1846–1912 **Nationality:** American **Location:** New York, NY, United States **Date Completed:** 1902 **Style|Movement:** Neoclassical

The title of the World's Columbian Exposition in Chicago in 1893 may have referred back 400 years to Columbus's journey to the New World, but it was forward-looking in terms of architecture. The director of works was Daniel Burnham, a successful Chicago architect, whose 'White City' fair buildings introduced the City Beautiful planning movement and showed off the work of a range of American architectural firms including McKim, Mead & White as well as Adler & Sullivan (with help from a youthful Frank Lloyd Wright), all set in Frederick Law Olmsted's landscaped surroundings. A few years later in New York City, Burnham was commissioned to design the Fuller Building on a triangular site at the junction of Broadway and Fifth Avenue. His vision of a 22-storey skyscraper in Renaissance palazzo style with Beaux-Arts detailing sounds bizarre, but he pulled it off and created a much-loved New York landmark, universally known as the Flatiron Building. Other celebrated projects followed, notably Washington's Union Station (1908). Here he used the Roman triumphal arch and giant Ionic columns as his signature theme, giving the terminus a statuesque grandeur. Burnham became head of the American Institute of Architects and owned the world's largest architectural firm, providing a business model for others. **SF**

Burton Decimus

Dates: 1800–81   **Nationality:** English   **Location:** Kew Gardens, Surrey, England   **Date Completed:** 1848   **Style|Movement:** Early Modernist

Tenth child of architect James Burton, the numerically named Decimus Burton was to prove more professionally prolific than his father. After beginning his training in the family firm, Burton came of age under the great John Nash, designing a slew of fashionable neoclassical buildings in and around London's parks and the south coast seaside towns. His works were not all for human habitation: he designed several structures for London Zoo, including the lofty Giraffe House in 1837, which remains one of the few listed buildings that still meets the stringent welfare standards for its intended occupants. Burton's greatest works were at Kew, where he designed the majestic Palm House with the aid of the Irish iron-founder, Richard Turner. The graceful arching structure with its high open spans for the unhindered spread of foliage was made possible by Turner's advanced wrought-iron construction and his ability to manufacture curved glass panels of unprecedented size. At 30 m (100 ft) wide and 20 m (66 ft) high, this technical marvel was the largest greenhouse of its day, its tropical contents kept verdant by a hot water heating system housed beneath iron gratings. Few architects have designed so successfully for both flora and fauna. **PC**

Butterfield William

Dates: 1814–1900 **Nationality:** English **Location:** Oxford University, Oxfordshire, England **Date Completed:** 1883 **Style | Movement:** Gothic Revival

Architecture offers a window into the minds of those who make it, and Keble College Chapel is no exception. An outstanding example of Victorian Gothic Revival, it was the work of the devout William Butterfield, who was born to non-conformist Protestant parents but came under the influence of the reactionary Cambridge Camden Society. Founded in 1839, the mission of this society of Cambridge undergraduates was to promote medieval gothic church architecture in place of neoclassical or Georgian models. The theology underpinning this enthusiasm was connected to the Oxford Movement within the Anglican Church, which sought to reinstate much of the colourful Catholic pomp and ritual that had been gradually stripped out since the Reformation. Butterfield's bold application of polychrome brickwork was viewed as the righteous antidote to monochrome Puritan facades. Ironically it was the railways, that most potent symbol of progress, which allowed Butterfield to indulge his love of colour. Before cheap transportation, architects were restricted to the local brick, made from local clays, but it was now possible to compose in a striking palette of Staffordshire blues, Kentish reds and yellow London stocks. Butterfield may have turned a blind eye, but this underlying modernity slyly subverted the medieval mission of his architecture. **PC**

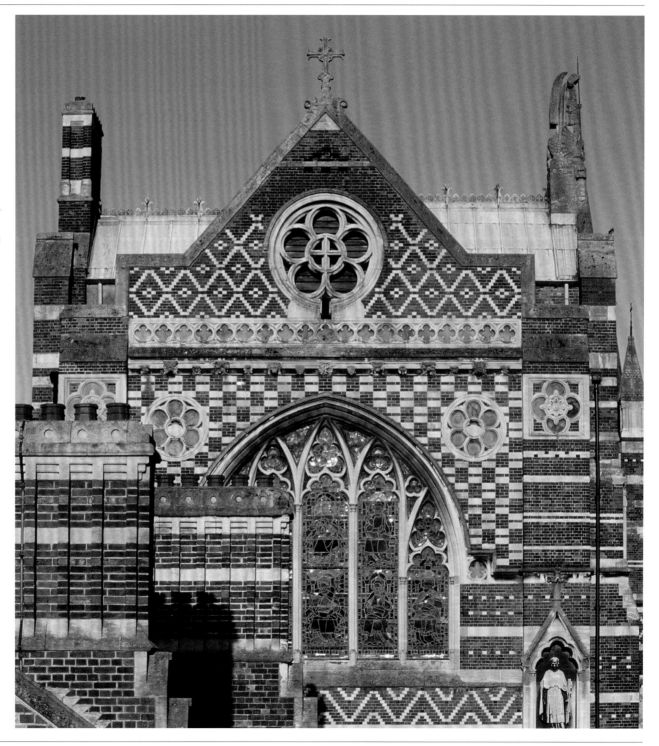

Calatrava Santiago

Dates: Born 1951   **Nationality:** Spanish   **Location:** Valencia, Spain   **Date Completed:** 2005   **Style | Movement:** Biomorphic

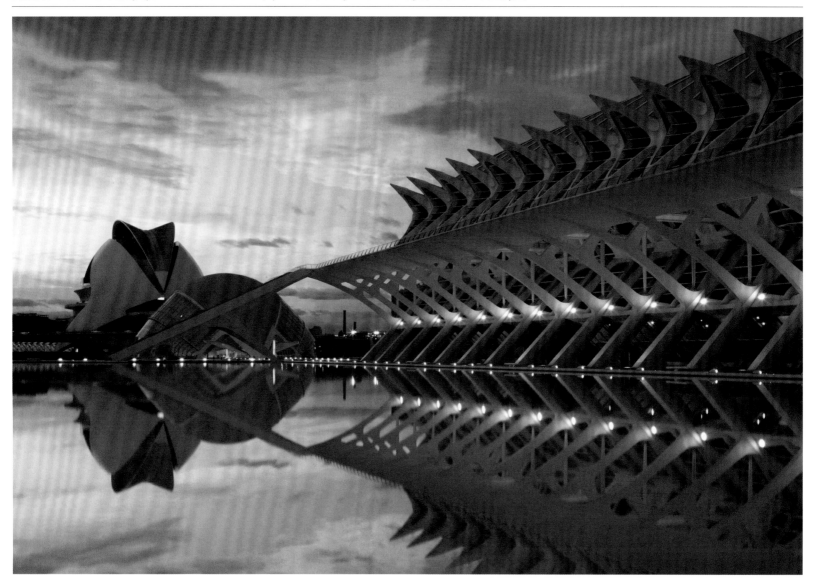

'Anything one man can imagine, other men can make real.' Jules Verne's assertion pithily captures the typical relationship between architects and engineers. Art and science often clash when converting concept into reality, but Santiago Calatrava is uniquely qualified in both spheres. He followed an undergraduate degree in architecture and a post-grad degree in urbanism from Valencia with a further degree and a doctorate in engineering from Zurich, creating an enviable double skill set that allows him to realize his visions without compromise. He is also a keen sculptor and painter with a recurring obsession with the human form, and all these facets of his personality can be seen in the principal buildings that dominate the City of Arts and Sciences in Valencia. Built along the dried bed of the diverted river Turia, the complex resembles a Verne-like fantasy landscape with shallow reflecting pools multiplying the slender concrete ribs of the science museum, behind which wink the folding eyelid louvres of the planetarium and the converging cranial plates of the Palace of the Arts. All share the same biomorphic DNA, realized in highly engineered concrete, steel and glass. When it comes to delivering his ideas, Calatrava is definitely his own man. **PC**

Cardinal Douglas

Dates: Born 1934   **Nationality:** Canadian   **Location:** Gatineau, Quebec, Canada   **Date Completed:** 1989   **Style | Movement:** Contemporary Modern

Buildings can attain the status of national symbols, but the Canadian Museum of Civilization was purpose-fully designed to represent the country on many levels. Douglas Cardinal responded to the curators' ambition of documenting 20,000 years of Canadian history with a composition reaching back to the last Ice Age. His treatment was topographic, dividing the complex into two distinct landforms: a curatorial wing containing laboratories, workshops and staff offices, and a public wing housing the galleries, theatres and museum. The facades of native Tyndall limestone have a particularly rich seam of meaning, reimagining the geology of the Canadian Shield, where the bedrock was first scarred by the grind-ing force of glaciers and then undercut by torrents of water as they melted. Cardinal's own Aboriginal ancestry informed other indigenous design references, including earthen lodges and wooden long houses, which all conform to the building's low silhouette in order to preserve views to the parliament across the river. Cardinal's office was the world's first architectural practice to become comput-erized, due to the demands of the complex curvilinear forms that dominate his work. The contradiction between the organic inspiration for his art and the man-made technol-ogy he must use to replicate it only reinforces the genius of nature's own designs. **PC**

Dates: 1723–96 **Nationality:** Scottish **Location:** London, England **Date Completed:** 1801 **Style | Movement:** Neo-Palladian

William Chambers worked in the neo-Palladian style after having to abandon his preferred—but unfashionable—French neoclassical designs to attract clients. After extensive foreign travel and architectural training in Paris and Italy, he became architectural tutor to Frederick, Prince of Wales (later George III) in 1755 and was soon sent to help Princess Augusta at Kew Palace. Chambers enjoyed considerable royal patronage, sharing the post of Comptroller of the King's Works, and in

1782 he became Surveyor-General. Alongside his royal work he ran a private practice specializing in grand country houses. Chambers was the second choice of architect for the work of the rebuilding of Somerset House after the existing Tudor palace was demolished in 1775. A new building was required for government offices and the main learned societies—the Royal Academy of Arts, the Royal Society and the Society of Antiquaries. He was told to provide 'a great public building ... an object

of national splendour'. In response he designed a quadrangular arrangement of essentially six-storey town houses that reached down to the Thames (for the Navy Office), giving each office a vertical slice of the building. Plain on the inside, the exterior was lavishly decorated. Chambers died before the complex project was completed. **SF**

Chareau Pierre

Rue St. Guillaume, La Maison de Verre | House of Glass

Dates: 1883–1950 **Nationality:** French **Location:** Paris, France **Date Completed:** 1932 **Style | Movement:** Modernist

Many inter-war medical practitioners extolled the powers of fresh air and light and Pierre Chareau's revolutionary Maison de Verre delivers both in abundance. Chareau was commissioned by Dr Jean Dalsace to construct a combined home and surgery on the site of an eighteenth-century courtyard house that he had intended to demolish. When one elderly tenant refused to move out, the resourceful Chareau cunningly inserted a steel frame to support the top floor flat, then gutted everything below, leaving a skeleton for a modern dwelling beneath. Chareau had trained as a draughtsman before working extensively as a furniture and interior designer, and he approached the house with an eye for the details. With the help of architect Bernard Bijvoet and craft metalworker Louis Dalbet he devised an amazingly flexible interior filled with sliding screens, metal furniture and a system of ducts and louvres that drew air into the building. The triple-height living room is flooded with natural light by day, while assuming the guise of lantern at night thanks to its floor-to-ceiling facade constructed from glass blocks, a recent invention. Frequently cited as an inspiration by modern architects, including Richard Rogers, there remains a healthy respect for Chareau's glowing masterpiece. **PC**

Dates: 1900–96 **Nationality:** German **Location:** Bexhill-on-Sea, England **Date Completed:** 1935 **Style | Movement:** Modernist

Religious intolerance in mainland Europe has caused many members of the avant-garde to make Britain their home. Born to wealthy Jewish parents, Serge Chermayeff emigrated from Russia as a boy in 1910. After completing his education he first worked for the furniture company of Willow & Garing, before qualifying as an architect and going into partnership with his friend, Erich Mendelsohn, who had fled to England to escape the Nazis in 1933. The Jewish duo soon met with success, winning the competition to design a cultural pavilion in Bexhill-on-Sea. Envisaged as a unique tourist attraction for the public's education and entertainment, the project was instigated by the town's mayor, the 9th Earl De La Warr, who supplied the land as well as his name. The slender cantilevered concrete lines of the De La Warr Pavilion were something foreign and exciting, pricking the interest of many young English architects. The first building in Britain to be constructed around a welded steel frame, its structure permitted the non-load-bearing walls to be made entirely of glass, bringing sun and sea air flooding into the interior. Beautifully restored to its thirties glory, this modernist beach head remains a stylish reminder of how immigrant talent has enriched Britain's architectural heritage. **PC**

Chipperfield David

Dates: Born 1953   **Nationality:** English   **Location:** Valencia, Spain   **Date Completed:** 2006   **Style | Movement:** Contemporary Modern

One of the most successful contemporary architects, London-based Sir David Chipperfield works in an uncompromisingly modernist style. After early success in Japan and consolidation in Europe, many of his more recent commissions have been in the United States. Chipperfield has become something of a public building specialist, having designed the River and Rowing Museum in Henley-on-Thames, the Neues Museum in Berlin and the Figge Art Museum in Iowa, among others. In addition to his

practice, Chipperfield is a teacher and has held professorships in both Europe and the United States. In the new millennium Chipperfield won the exciting challenge to design the America's Cup Building in the industrial port of Valencia, Spain. The result, which was designed and built in a mere 11 months, was the Veles e Vents (Sails and Winds) building. Unmistakably nautical in inspiration—it is also called the Foredeck Building—it showcases four horizontal white stacked and shifted parallel 'wings', which

provide shade for onlookers, coupled with an uninterrupted panorama of the seascape. These concrete levels surround each floor and cantilever out to become huge viewing decks made from Brazilian timber decking—some 60 per cent of the building is outside space. Both architect and building have, unsurprisingly, been lauded with architectural and design prizes. **SF**

Coates Wells

Dates: 1895–1958 **Nationality:** Canadian **Location:** Belsize Park, London, England **Date Completed:** 1934 **Style|Movement:** Modernist

Travel is said to broaden the mind, and few minds have covered as many miles or creative disciplines as Wells Coates. Born to Canadian missionaries overseas, he lived in Japan for 15 years before embarking on a grand world tour with his father and tutor, exploring India, China, Egypt and Europe. After studying engineering in Vancouver and London, Coates took a job as a sub-editor for the *Daily Express,* before branching out in 1928 to design a series of crisp modernist shop interiors for Crysede Silks, all executed in glass, plywood and steel. Heavily involved with the BBC's new recording studios, Coates also understood the listeners' perspective, designing the EKO AD65 radio whose circular Bakelite construction has made it an icon of 1930s design. His shop fitting impressed Jack and Molly Pritchard of furniture company Isokon, who commissioned Coates to design a block of flats to embody their shared ideas on modern living. Built with reinforced concrete and wrapped with streamlined stairs and balconies, the building's compact flats echo ship's cabins with their efficient built-in furniture. At one time home to such luminaries as Agatha Christie, Marcel Breuer and Walter Gropius, its resemblance to a landlocked ocean-liner make it an apt monument to Coates's well-travelled genius. **PC**

Cockerell Charles Robert

Dates: 1788–1863 **Nationality:** English **Location:** Liverpool, England **Date Completed:** 1854 **Style|Movement:** Neoclassical

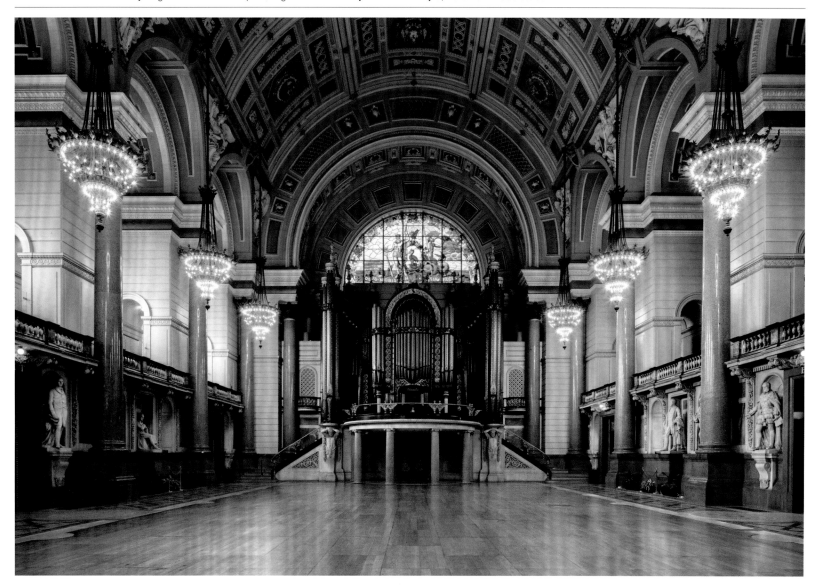

Charles Cockerell initially wanted to be an archaeologist. After early architectural training, he studied Ancient Greek buildings *in situ* for seven years before reluctantly returning to architectural practice at the age of 29. To the irritation of his father—who had trained Cockerell to follow in his footsteps—he refused to be commercial and insisted on becoming a 'professor of the beautiful in architecture'. Cockerell devised his own architectural language, combining classical Greek with sixteenth- and seventeenth-century Italian architecture and the English Baroque of Sir Christopher Wren, Sir John Vanbrugh and Nicholas Hawksmoor. Many of his domestic commissions have gone but some work survives in grand public buildings such as the Ashmolean Museum in Oxford and bank branch offices in London, Manchester, Plymouth, Bristol and Liverpool, designed in his capacity as surveyor for the Bank of England. In 1851 Cockerell was asked to complete St George's Hall in Liverpool, for which an interior was needed. He designed one of the largest barrel-vaulted ceilings in the country, held up by columns of polished red granite over an elaborate floor of over 30,000 Minton tiles. Cockerell was a highly sophisticated and fastidious architect who would not compromise his ideas to pander to the latest fad for Gothic Revival, and so faded into the architectural background in his final years. **SF**

Connell Amyas

Dates: 1901–80 **Nationality:** New Zealander **Location:** Amersham, Buckinghamshire, England **Date Completed:** 1931 **Style | Movement:** Modernist

Soaring above its chalky hillside site, wings out-stretched to receive the sun, the former home of Professor Bernard Ashmole is regarded as the first truly modernist building to be built in Britain by a British architect, despite the fact that he was born in New Zealand. Amyas Connell began his training in Wellington before working his passage to England as a stoker on a steamer alongside future colleague Basil Ward. The talented young Connell studied at the Bartlett School in London, winning the coveted Rome Scholarship in 1926, then travelling to the British School in Rome where his eye was caught not only by the ruins he was measuring but also by the angular concrete mass of early modernist build-ings by designers including Le Corbusier. Having studied two styles at either end of recorded history, Connell returned to England and formed a practice with Australian architect Stewart Lloyd Thomson before being asked to design a family home for Ashmole, the former Director of the British School.

Connell fused the essence of classical planning with twentieth-century material sciences, supporting his Y-shaped plan with a reinforced concrete frame, in-filled with brick and plaster. Though claiming inspiration both ancient and modern, High & Over also has its roots Down Under. **PC**

Cook Peter

Dates: Born 1936   **Nationality:** English   **Location:** Graz, Austria   **Date Completed:** 2003   **Style | Movement:** Biomorphic

With colourful montages of a technologically advanced society, the architectural collective Archigram offered a rebellious antidote to the bland modernism that characterized post-war British architecture. Formed by like-minded young London architects in the early sixties, its work fused consumer culture, new materials and space-age modular tech-nologies to create futuristic scenarios for human survival. Founder member Sir Peter Cook's famous 1964 design for a 'Plug-in City' was typical of the Archigram ethos; it had living cells that could be moved around a giant megastructure by crane and plugged in wherever resources were available. Though their work proved iconic and influ-ential, the youthful members of Archigram were largely unable to turn fantasy into reality. Some forty years later, Cook was given a rare opportunity to do so, with the Kunsthaus Graz, designed with fellow Bartlett teacher Colin Fournier. The centrepiece of Graz's tenure as European City of Culture, the 'Friendly Alien', as it is known, forms a dark, dramatic contrast to the pastel-toned Baroque buildings that it looks poised to envelop. Its conventional concrete core and steel frame structure are skinned with a membrane of thick acrylic panels, erupting into 16 nozzles across its roofline that act as light wells for the galleries inside. With its retro-sixties space-age aesthetic, the Kunsthaus is yesterday's tomorrow, today. **PC**

Cubitt Thomas

Dates: 1788–1855 **Nationality:** English **Location:** Isle of Wight, England **Date Completed:** 1851 **Style | Movement:** Italianate

Much of central London would not look as it does today if it were not for Thomas Cubitt, one of the great speculative builders of the early nineteenth century. His buildings created much of Belgravia, Chelsea, Pimlico, Islington and Clapham—with Eaton Square being the jewel. He was a pioneer who believed in providing public parks and lobbied for the extension of the Thames Embankment as well as for a proper sewerage and drainage system for London. A builder as well as an architect, he employed large numbers of tradesmen and looked after their welfare, providing his workers with equipment and facilities including a lending library. His obituary in the 1857 Minutes of the Proceedings of the Institution of Civil Engineers recognized his idealism and called them 'the real friend of the working man'. He also had friends in high places and helped Prince Albert to design Osborne House. Knocking down the original Georgian house, Cubitt built an Italianate villa with towers and grand interiors all set in formal gardens. Unsurprisingly, having worked so well with Albert, he then won the contract to extend Buckingham Palace along the east front. This entailed moving Nash's Marble Arch, which had been at the entrance to the palace, to its new position at the northeastern corner of Hyde Park. He also helped persuade Prince Albert that London should hold a Great Exhibition. **SF**

Cullinan Edward

Dates: Born 1931 **Nationality:** English **Location:** Weald & Downland Museum, Sussex, England **Date Completed:** 2002 **Style | Movement:** Eco-Modernism

Despite beginning his career detailing hard concrete monoliths under Sir Denys Lasdun, Edward 'Ted' Cullinan has developed an altogether softer, more eco-conscious architecture, which displays great sensitivity to site, landscape and context. Having designed visitor centres for major world heritage sites, he received his greatest acclaim for a functional workshop whose popularity threatens to upstage the heritage it conserves. Set within the rolling West Sussex countryside, the Weald &

Downland Open Air Museum offers a window onto five centuries of wooden buildings, the majority of which arrived in component form, ready to be restored in rudimentary workshops. National Lottery funding made it possible to erect a purpose-built facility and the enlightened client saw this as an opportunity to enrich the history of the subject. Nestling like an immense peanut shell amongst the trees, the Gridshell's undulating cedar cladding cloaks a novel lightweight frame constructed from

36 m (120 ft)-long green oak lathes. Four loosely clamped layers of these lathes were perched on top of a scaffold, 2.5 m (8 ft) above floor level. As the scaffolding was gradually removed, gravity acted as a sculptor and the lathes gracefully bent down to form the gridshell. Cullinan was once again working in harmony with nature. **PC**

Davis Alexander Jackson

Dates: 1803–92 **Nationality:** American **Location:** New York, NY, United States **Date Completed:** 1842 **Style|Movement:** Greek Revival

The leading American architect of the era before the Civil War, New Yorker Alexander Davis styled himself an 'Architectural Composer'. Working alone, Davis was a successful designer of grand country houses. Working with his partner, Ithiel Town, Davis generally designed in elegant Greek Revival style with occasional diversions into Gothic Revival. As Town and Davis they comprised the first properly professional architectural firm in the United States and designed the Greek Revival North Carolina State Capitol in Raleigh. Davis found a lot of work in North Carolina with the university as well as at the huge Hospital for the Insane, where he insisted on indoor plumbing and gas lighting. In 1832 Town and Davis won the commission for the New York Customs House (since 1955 named the Federal Hall National Memorial) to be placed on the site of the old Federal Hall on Wall Street—the building where George Washington was inaugurated as president and which served as the first United States Capitol. Built in Greek Revival style with Westchester marble, it was the first customs house in America and took over ten years to build. Its huge temple frontage, since 1883 graced by a statue of Washington, is today dwarfed by skyscrapers but remains a powerful piece of architecture. **SF**

Delorme Philibert (also de L'Orme)   Château de Chenonceau extension

Dates: c.1514–70   **Nationality:** French   **Location:** Chenonceau, France   **Date Completed:** 1559, bridge (1576, gallery)   **Style | Movement:** Gothic / Early Renaissance

The greatest architect of the French Renaissance, Philibert Delorme worked for Francis I, Henri II and Charles IX, as well as for various high church patrons including Pope Paul III. For the French kings he worked on Fontainebleau, Saint-Germain-en-Laye and the tomb for Francis I at Saint-Denis; for the queen mother Catherine de'Medici, the Tuileries; and for Diane de Poitiers (Henri II's mistress), the Château d'Anet. The son of a stonemason, his architectural style was greatly influenced by the works of the Italian Renaissance but Delorme altered it to reflect French sensibilities, materials and above all, elegance, to produce a French Renaissance style altogether lighter and more restrained than the original. Many of his buildings have not survived, but some of his greatest work is to be seen at Chenonceau. The main block of the chateau was begun in 1515; by 1547 it belonged to Diane de Poitiers who commissioned Delorme to design a covered bridge to link the existing building to the left bank of the River Cher. Delorme designed a sophisticated five-arch bridge in French Renaissance style. The two-storey gallery above was later commissioned by Catherine de'Medici from Jean Bullant. **SF**

Dates: 1884–1974 **Nationality:** Dutch **Location:** Hilversum, Utrecht, Netherlands **Date Completed:** 1931 **Style|Movement:** Modernist

Standing tall and fortress-like behind a moat of lake and gardens, Hilversum's town hall possesses a clean, hard, martial character. Despite the visual parallels with Piet Mondrian's De Stijl paintings, its architect shared none of that movement's ideology, saving his admiration for the brick-built Prairie houses of Frank Lloyd Wright. Willem Marinus Dudok trained at the Royal Military Academy in Breda, where he was schooled in the art of fortifications, for which brick was a major material. Having served as an engineer, he left the forces in 1913, taking the post of Temporary Director of Public Work in Leiden, before becoming the City Architect for the small town of Hilversum in 1928. In command of the town's civic infrastructure, Dudok designed many new public buildings and even entire neighbourhoods before tackling the prominent structure of the town hall itself. Handling his chosen material with military precision, he transformed vast plains of brick into elegant, asymmetrical compositions, cut with dark shadows and edged in black tiles. This love of controlled order even ran to the regimented yellow bricks themselves, of which 680,000 were produced for this project alone. Made to his precise specifications, they are known as Hilversum bricks to this day. **PC**

Dunster Bill

Dates: Born 1960   **Nationality:** English   **Location:** Wallington, Surrey, England   **Date Completed:** 2002   **Style|Movement:** Eco-Modernism

Carbon emissions are a global issue, one that invites local solutions. In Britain, the built environment accounts for 25 per cent of carbon emissions compared to aviation's 5.5 per cent – a fact largely unscrutinized by the media. While volume house-builders remain indifferent, the philanthropic Peabody Trust commissioned architect Bill Dunster to design a zero energy development (ZED) of 99 homes that might meet the ideal of carbon-neutral living. Dunster had worked on the green aspects of several high-profile projects, including Portcullis House in Westminster, in his 14 years as an associate of Michael Hopkins. His holistic approach at BedZED factored in the energy used to produce and transport materials, which were largely sourced from within a 56 km (35 mile) radius. The intelligent north-south orientation of the terraced houses harnesses passive solar gain and strong natural light. Banks of photovoltaic cells in triple-glazed facades harvest more renewable energy, while the roofs are populated by colourful cock's comb ventilators: part of a heat exchange system that recycles the warmth of the air being exhaled. Though the community's energy consumption is 10 per cent that of an equivalent development conforming to 1995 building regulations, BedZED regrettably remains a hopeful prototype, waiting for a conservative housing industry to wake up and smell the carbon. **PC**

Eames Charles and Ray

Eames House | Case Study House No. 8

Dates: 1907–78 (Charles); 1912–88 (Ray) **Nationality:** American **Location:** Pacific Palisades, Los Angeles, United States **Date Completed:** 1949 **Style | Movement:** Modernist

Industrial components and domestic bliss may not seem like natural partners, but the iconic Eames House is a monument to two designers and their ability to humanize modernity. Nestling unassumingly like an abstract Mondrian painting behind a screen of eucalyptus trees, the long-time home and studio of Charles and Ray Eames was where they worked on everything from films and furniture to graphics and industrial design. Created as part of the famous Case Study House programme sponsored by *Arts & Architecture Magazine*, the initial 1945 plan by Charles and his friend Eero Saarinen envisaged a steel and glass box cantilevered over the sloping wooded plot. Despite selecting only prefabricated steel components from catalogues, the post-war materials shortage led to a three-year delay in delivery and during this long gestation period the Eameses totally revised their plans to preserve the trees and setting. With its grid-like frame dividing panels of pure colour, the house is effectively an enlargement of the freestanding steel and plywood storage units they were then designing for Vitra, and was fabricated in a matter of days. The couple proceeded to fill it with art and artefacts they had collected on their travels around the world, creating a rich, stimulating environment that still defines casual, modern living. **PC**

Eiffel Alexandre Gustave

Dates: 1832–1923   **Nationality:** French   **Location:** Paris, France   **Date Completed:** 1889   **Style | Movement:** Early Modernist

Few people have had the skill and talent to design an iconic structure that defines a nation. Gustave Eiffel is the only person responsible for two: the Eiffel Tower and the Statue of Liberty. Hailing from the provincial town of Dijon, young Eiffel specialized in engineering with a focus on bridgework, using his skill with mathematics to design ever lighter and stronger metalwork. By 1867 his reputation secured him the commission for the arched Gallery of Machines for the Paris Exhibition. When the great engineer Viollet-le-Duc died while working on the Statue of Liberty in 1879, Eiffel was made the project's chief engineer. He drew up plans for a revolutionary new metal skeletal support structure for the copper skin. This was created from the ground up in Paris, disassembled and shipped to New York, where his team put it together again. For the 1889 Universal Exposition in Paris, Eiffel was charged with creating its totemic symbol. The Eiffel Tower was a pioneering feat of structural engineering, not least for its strength and wind resistance. At 300 m (984 ft), it was the tallest structure in the world and contained 12,000 different components. Remarkably, however, if it were melted down, the metal would fill its footprint to only 6.5 cm (2.5 in). **SF**

Eisenman Peter — Memorial to the Murdered Jews of Europe | Field of Stelae

Dates: Born 1932   **Nationality:** American   **Location:** Berlin, Germany   **Date Completed:** 2005   **Style | Movement:** Deconstructivist

Peter Eisenman remains a provocative figure within the architectural world, which he permeates through his extensive writing, theorizing, teaching and curating. Designed with Richard Troot and Laurie Olin and opened in 1989, his Wexner Center at Ohio State University was the first major public building in the Deconstructivist style. Eisenman has been accused of being more focused on theory than practice and the building, which demonstrated his ideas on liberating the discipline of architecture by rejecting functionalism, became a byword for architectural disfunctionality, with poorly specified materials, disorientating interiors and strong sunlight in spaces intended for hanging art. This atmosphere is perhaps more appropriate for a monument recording an epic case of inhumanity, the competition for which Eisenman won in 1997. A stele is an upright stone, usually used in a memorial or commemorative context, and Eisenman's Field of Stelae in Berlin fills some 19,000 m^2 (4.7 acres) with a grid of concrete oblongs that have an equal area, but varying heights. The stated intention was for visitors walking through this sloping, repetitive landscape to find themselves immersed in a confusing, unsettling atmosphere, symbolic of an orderly system of society losing touch with reason. Though highly controversial throughout its construction, this Holocaust memorial attracted over 3.5 million visitors in its first year alone. **PC**

Erskine Ralph

Dates: 1914–2005 **Nationality:** English / Swedish **Location:** London, England **Date Completed:** 1992 **Style | Movement:** Contemporary Modern

Ralph Erskine's socialist ideals and his Quaker faith were fundamental to his architectural philosophy. As a result, he insisted that his buildings had to be compatible with the landscape they would inhabit as well as suited to the uses and needs of the people who would occupy them. Erskine settled in Sweden in 1935 and spent much of his professional career working just outside Stockholm. He admired the work of the Functionalist Swedish architects who put their government's social-welfare political outlook into material form. His signature style balances light and heavy elements against each other in a variety of forms and materials and brought thoughtful design to many low-cost housing projects, including in the 1960s the redevelopment for social housing of Newcastle's council-owned Byker slum district. Years later, Swedish developers commissioned Erskine to design The Ark, a large ship-like, dark-skinned office building sitting beside the A4 overpass at Hammersmith. Inside—particularly since its 2006 refit by DN-A—it is bright and airy, illuminated with natural roof-lit spaces, especially through the vast floor-to-roof atrium around which run large communal areas and walkways. Erskine's final achievement was devising the winning scheme for the development of the Greenwich Millennium Village in 1997. **SF**

Farrell Terry

The Deep

Dates: Born 1938   **Nationality:** English   **Location:** Hull, East Yorkshire, England   **Date Completed:** 2002   **Style|Movement:** Postmodern

With an impressive portfolio encompassing architecture, master planning and urban design, Sir Terry Farrell is one of the most prolific British architects of his generation, both at home and overseas. Since founding his own practice in 1980, Farrell has delivered bold designs for everything from international airports and government offices to rowing clubs and railway stations. Something of an architectural chameleon, his style has constantly changed to suit his brief, though his eclectic output in the eighties

and nineties came to define British postmodernism. His work is often integral to its occupant's public identity, from the giant egg cup finials on the Camden base of breakfast broadcaster TV-AM (1983) to the imposing Mayan-style ziggurat of the MI6 headquarters at Vauxhall Cross (1994), star of many James Bond films. One of his most successful compositions is a major regeneration scheme for post-industrial Hull, featuring a major aquarium with a 10 m (33 ft)-deep tank. Named The Deep, it was

conceived as a slice of the ocean floor being driven to the surface by tectonic forces, exposing the fossilized history it contains, though there are many other appropriate maritime metaphors including sharks and super tankers. A resounding popular success, Farrell's bespoke narrative has given Hull a much-needed modern face. **PC**

Foster Norman

Dates: Born 1935   **Nationality:** English   **Location:** London, England   **Date Completed:** 2003   **Style|Movement:** High Tech

Recipient of practically every major architectural award, Norman Foster has reached the pinnacle of his profession by pursuing finely engineered solutions that are the epitome of High Tech design. His first skyscraper, the Hong Kong & Shanghai Bank (1986), was a highly original composition that rejected a conventional layout of central concrete cores in favour of an immense steel frame of eight masts linked by huge girders from which the floor plates were suspended. Flexible and column-free, these floors were filled with natural light and offered stunning views across the harbour. Completed 28 years later, the ballistic monolith of 30 St Mary Axe demonstrates how Foster and his team have continued to push the boundaries of high-rise technology with the help of computer-aided design. Built for another financial institution, the reinsurers Swiss Re, the spiralling glazing of the tower's elegant diamond lattice exoskeleton expresses its ingenious energy-saving ventilation system, which harnesses natural convection to draw air up through the building. With the structure externalized, Foster had again created a light-filled, open plan office space, with exceptional views and a coveted penthouse restaurant at its apex. Foster's office has proved a fertile environment for decades of cutting-edge design, but his Stirling prize-winning 'Gherkin' will remain a highpoint. **PC**

Dates: 1823–65 **Nationality:** English **Location:** London, England **Date Completed:** 1871 **Style | Movement:** Renaissance Revival

The British Army was kept busy in the nineteenth century as the empire expanded to cover a quarter of the globe. Postings to far-flung places encouraged the forces to be self-sufficient, training their own Royal Engineers to secure land through railways, roads and architecture. Captain Francis Fowke was a member of this capable officer class, able to design for both war and peace. Having served with distinction in Bermuda and Paris, he was assigned

the task of designing several government projects, including the National Gallery of Ireland and the Royal Museum in Edinburgh. He also laid out the Royal Albert Hall but, like its namesake, he would not see it completed, dying suddenly from a burst blood vessel aged only 42. The hall was finished by a fellow officer, then Lieutenant-Colonel Henry Y. D. Scott, who followed Fowkes's elliptical plan but was largely responsible for the terracotta and Fareham Red

brick exterior. The imposing glass and wrought iron dome was engineered by Rowland Mason Ordish, but its poor acoustics were not solved for almost a century, when fibreglass diffusers were installed. This detail did little to diminish the hall's popularity and it remains proof that soldiers can forge things more enduring than empires. **PC**

Fuksas Massimiliano

Dates: Born 1944   **Nationality:** Italian   **Location:** Milan, Italy   **Date Completed:** 2005   **Style | Movement:** Contemporary Modern

Massimiliano Fuksas originally wanted to be a poet or an artist. It was only in his twenties that he came to his work in architecture, which he describes as essentially simple forms on a grand scale. In partnership with his wife Doriana Mandrelli, Fuksas deploys these bold elements to solve develop-mental challenges; they are experts in large urban complexes and public works. To this end they have worked across Europe and in China and Japan. In

their home country of Italy, they were commissioned to design a new complex for the FieraMilano, one of the oldest and the most important trade fairs in Italy. Its old site in the centre of Milan had became too cramped and a new location was chosen just west of the city. The result was one of the world's foremost venues: eight pavilions with a total of 345,000 m^2 (3.7 million sq ft) of covered exhibition space with a further 60,000 m^2 (650,000 sq ft) of outdoor space.

Over the vast main building, Fuksas draped a canopy of triangular-shaped glass and steel, which flows like fabric over the skeletal steel supports and creates large cone-like skylights that echo the distant Alps lurking on the horizon. Fuksas also teaches his architectural philosophies at numerous universities. **SF**

Fuller Richard Buckminster

Biosphere

Dates: 1895–1983 **Nationality:** American **Location:** Île Sainte-Hélène, Montreal, Canada **Date Completed:** 1967 **Style | Movement:** High Tech

A modern polymath with a flair for self-promotion, Richard Buckminster Fuller was to influence a generation of High Tech designers. Having failed to graduate from Harvard, Fuller married at 22 and then enlisted in the United States Navy in 1917, serving as a communications officer and gunboat commander. He credited his technical expertise to his naval service and much of his future output would express the martial preoccupations with speed, lightness and strength. Fuller's efficient 'more

for less' design philosophy was encapsulated by the compound term 'Dymaxion', which he applied to everything from teardrop shaped three-wheeled cars to lightweight hexagonal houses sheathed in duraluminium. Much of Fuller's work remained as prototypes, but his patented system of geodesic construction found widespread applications from arid deserts to polar regions. The most imposing example was built to house the United States Pavilion at Montreal's Expo '67. Despite having

a diameter of almost 76 m (250 ft), the structure weighed just 800 tonnes, covering the maximum area for the minimum material without the need for scaffolding. The original skin of translucent acrylic-glass panels was consumed by fire in 1976, but the skeletal dome has since become home to a succession of environmental-themed museums, continuing to provide more with even less. **PC**

Gabriel Ange-Jacques

Château of the Petit Trianon

Dates: 1698–1782   **Nationality:** French   **Location:** Versailles, France   **Date Completed:** 1768   **Style | Movement:** Neoclassical

Ange-Jacques Gabriel was the son of the *Premier Architecte* at the royal palace of Versailles. In 1742, after working as his father's principal assistant, Gabriel succeeded him as the most important architect in France, working directly for King Louis XV over the next 40 years. Gabriel produced symmetrical, classically proportioned buildings, most notably at Versailles but also for the north side of the Place Louis XV (now Place de la Concorde) in 1772. True to Enlightenment ideals, Gabriel believed that

architectural progress, as with all else, depended on discipline and reason. The work for which he is most celebrated is the Petit Trianon in the grounds of Versailles, built for Louis XV's mistress Madame de Pompadour. Surrounded by gardens, each side of the cube-shaped building is different (the southeastern side and the main courtyard are shown here). It is a fine example of the transition between the early eighteenth-century rococo style and the more sophisticated Corinthian-influenced

neoclassical style, soon to be recognized as Style Louis XVI. Gone are the rococo embellishments of earlier buildings, replaced by elegant restraint and harmonious proportions. It is revered as one of the most perfect buildings in France. Unfortunately, the royal mistress died before the villa was finished and it was her successor, Madame du Barry, who first enjoyed it. **SF**

Garnier Jean-Louis Charles

Paris Opéra | Le Palais Garnier

Dates: 1825–98 **Nationality:** French **Location:** Paris, France **Date Completed:** 1874 **Style | Movement:** Beaux Arts

One of the most spectacular buildings in Paris, if not the whole of France, the flamboyant Palais Garnier is located on the Avenue de l'Opéra in the ninth *arondissement*; its designer, Jean-Louis Charles Garnier, was equally dramatic. After beginning his education in Paris, Garnier studied for five years in Rome at the Villa Medici. He returned home inspired by Roman pageantry and determined to bring all of that pomp and extravagance to his own buildings in a glorious marriage of architecture, ornament, painting and sculpture. Garnier considered his style to be a modern synthesis of earlier architectural forms brought up to date and combined with the latest technology. This was in accord with the prevailing mood of Napoleon III's Second Empire, which included a love of embellishment and luxury. To get the Opéra commission Garnier had to win a tough competition, which he did with a design that fitted comfortably into its location and surroundings and which was able to fulfil its intended function. It took 14 years to complete and, when finished, it was a triumph: a working theatre with a glittering, golden and sculpture-filled reception for the public and a behind-the-scenes arena at the back where theatrical staff could conjure their magic unhindered. **SF**

Gaudí Antoni (Antoni Gaudí i Cornet)

Dates: 1852–1926   **Nationality:** Spanish   **Location:** Barcelona, Spain   **Date Completed:** Unfinished   **Style|Movement:** Art Nouveau

Antoni Gaudí is inextricably associated with Barcelona and dominates the character of the city as very few other architects have achieved in any location. His architectural style can be described loosely as Art Nouveau, but even within that category it is atypical. Gaudí took his inspiration from the organic forms in nature, and his buildings twist and turn as if grown from concrete. His playful use of bright colours is also unusual among architects and shows up mostly in the form of ceramic tiles, which he used like mosaics. The city is dotted with his buildings, like exotic jewels sewn into a tapestry—Casa Vicens, Casa Calvet, Casa Milà and Casa Batlló as well as the palace of Güell, the Colonia Güell chapel and the monastery school for the Theresian order. However, it is for La Sagrada Família that he is best known. Originally funded by public subscription, this extraordinary organic cathedral will feature 18 tall towers when finished. It has been under construction since 1882 and is still being built: it is hoped it will be completed by 2041. For the last 15 years of his life Gaudí devoted himself to the building. He was a constant presence on site, modifying and adjusting his plans as the building progressed. **SF**

Dates: Born 1929   **Nationality:** Canadian / American   **Location:** Bilbao, Spain   **Date Completed:** 1997   **Style | Movement:** Deconstructivist

Not since the Sydney Opera House has a single building so definitively put a city on the world map. Frank Gehry's Guggenheim Museum in Bilbao transformed the fortunes of this Basque fishing port, making it a popular city-break destination in the age of low-cost flights and cultural tourism. Many architects have tried to emulate Gehry's success-ful formula, but few have been able to deliver it with such panache—and still stay on budget. The secret lay in Gehry's complete control of the design process, which he achieved by customizing the powerful software program CATIA, originally developed for the aerospace industry. Gehry's earlier work, though still filled with eccentric forms, had been constrained by his reliance on external engineers and contractors correctly interpreting his complex designs. With CATIA, he found the freedom to laser-scan his expressive sketch models of crumpled card and paper, and to use that digital data to make accurate technical drawings that could be broken down into costable component forms. The curvaceous steel frames supporting the Guggenheim's shimmering titanium skin retain Gehry's personal touch, making the gallery as much a work of art as its contents. Though he had already won the prestigious Pritzker Prize in 1989, it was the Guggenheim that made Gehry a global phenom-enon. **PC**

Gibberd Frederick Ernest

Liverpool Metropolitan Cathedral

Dates: 1908–94 **Nationality:** English **Location:** Liverpool, England **Date Completed:** 1967 **Style|Movement:** Modernist

The phrase 'standing on the shoulders of giants' could be applied quite literally to Liverpool's Catholic cathedral, for Frederick Gibberd's crown of concrete and steel sits upon a crypt of a far grander design. The Great Irish Famine of 1845–52 led to waves of Catholic immigrants arriving in Liverpool, and many opted to settle rather than sail to America. This enlarged congregation encouraged the clergy to commission a cathedral from Edwin Welby Pugin in 1853, but due to lack of funds only the Lady Chapel was completed. A new site was chosen in 1930 and Sir Edwin Lutyens designed what would have been the second-largest church in the world, with a dome taller than St Peter's in Rome. The work was funded by contributions from the city's Catholic working class but, again, ambition outstripped resources and the plan was abandoned in 1958 with only the crypt complete. Gibberd won the subsequent international competition for a more affordable solution, presenting a radically modern design whose circular plan and central altar allowed the 2,000-person congregation greater participation in the mass. Having made his reputation designing a succession of successful low-cost flats and housing developments, it is fitting that Gibberd should be the architect who delivered the cathedral the masses could afford. **PC**

Gibbs James

Dates: 1682–1754 **Nationality:** Scottish **Location:** Oxford, England **Date Completed:** 1749 **Style | Movement:** Mannerist

Unlike many of his contemporaries, James Gibbs was not a Palladian architect. He had a preference for the Baroque from his early training in Italy, but followed no particular rules and, although his chief influence was Sir Christopher Wren, is often described as a stylistic outsider. Gibbs designed St Mary-le-Strand and St Martin-in-the-Fields on the edge of Trafalgar Square as well as the Octagon at Orleans House in Twickenham. He also had a successful sideline designing religious monuments, often in collaboration with Alexander Pope, who wrote the epitaph, and Michael Rysbrack, who sculpted the monument. Horace Walpole said of him, 'His praise was fidelity to rules, his failing, want of grace.' Towards the end of his life Gibbs reluctantly accepted a commission to complete the Radcliffe Library to house the scientific library named after the Royal Physician Dr Radcliffe, who provided £40,000 for a 'Physic' library. After the original architect, Nicholas Hawksmoor, died, Gibbs was asked to work to the former's circular plan but went on to change much else, in particular losing Hawksmoor's plinth. Externally, the Camera is made up of three parts: the dome and cupola, containing eight windows, the Corinthian-columned upper floor and the eight-bayed heavily rusticated ground floor. In 1860 the Radcliffe Library was renamed the Radcliffe Camera (camera is 'room' in Latin) and became part of the Bodleian Library. **SF**

Goldfinger Ernö

Dates: 1902–87 **Nationality:** Hungarian **Location:** London, England **Date Completed:** 1972 **Style | Movement:** Brutalist

Ernö Goldfinger left Hungary after World War I and moved to Paris, where he studied architecture and became a fan of the early modernists such as Le Corbusier and, particularly, Auguste Perret. In the early 1930s he met and married an English heiress and moved to London. Post-war Britain needed rebuilding but money and resources were scarce. Slowly Goldfinger's bold urbanism started to win clients for offices, schools, homes and shops. Then, in 1959, he secured a huge commission from the Greater London Council to design the Elephant and Castle complex, but the concrete Brutalism of the scheme was almost universally hated. Goldfinger moved on to designing tower blocks, including the 11-storey Carradale House and 27-storey Balfron Tower, both in Tower Hamlets. His landmark building is the 31-floor Trellick Tower in North Kensington, with a reinforced concrete facade and a tower-shaped lift and service shaft. Trellick Tower was designed as an autonomous living unit with flats and maisonettes, launderettes, a doctor's surgery, shops, a nursery school, hobby rooms and an old people's club. The space intended to become a pub instead became Goldfinger's office. Initially, very few of the tenants were enamoured of the building, but today many people see it as a desirable place to live. **SF**

Graves Michael

Dates: Born 1934 **Nationality:** American **Location:** Burbank, CA, United States **Date Completed:** 1990 **Style|Movement:** Postmodernist

The personification of American postmodernism, Michael Graves remains a prolific designer of everything from kettles and tea caddies to corporate headquarters. Adherents to the postmodern (Po-mo) movement see modernism as a kind of aesthetic straitjacket, and strive to escape its restrictions and to imbue their buildings with greater meaning by borrowing freely from both history and popular culture. Graves's Team Disney Building manages to combine both impulses, by replacing the

stone caryatids (carved female statues sometimes used as supporting columns in Greek temples) with giant facsimiles of Disney's seven dwarves. Disney Studios was able to move to the Burbank site in large part due to the huge profits generated by the 1947 full-length animated feature, *Snow White and the Seven Dwarves*, in which the diminutive characters appeared, making their supporting role in this building particularly appropriate. Putting the 'heigh-ho' into Po-mo is typical of Graves's sense of humour

and his use of figurative elements: his best-selling Whistling Bird Kettle for Alessi (1985) has a plastic bird whistle perched on the spout. His profitable work for Alessi and American superstore Target has made Graves a household name for products and home wares, as well as architecture. Like Disney, he has learned the power of merchandising. **PC**

Greene Charles Sumner and Henry Mather   David Gamble House

Dates: 1868–1957 (Charles) and 1870–1954 (Henry)   **Nationality:** American   **Location:** Pasadena, CA, United States   **Date Completed:** 1909   **Style|Movement:** Arts and Crafts

A train journey changed the careers of Charles and Henry Greene, who produced one of the most revered examples of residential American Arts and Crafts design. The Greene brothers grew up largely in St Louis, Missouri, attending the Manual Training School of Washington University and graduating in wood and metal working in 1888. A classical training at MIT's School of Architecture followed, as did a series of apprenticeships with various practices in Boston. In 1892, their parents moved to Pasadena, California, and the next year they asked their sons to join them. Stopping off en route, the brothers visited the World's Columbian Exposition in Chicago, where they were greatly impressed by the traditional Japanese Ho-o-den pavilion. Charles had a second exposure to Japanese design at the 1904 Louisiana Purchase Exposition. These influences abound in the open-plan house commissioned by the wealthy soap-maker David Gamble. The Greenes emphasized construction details, with visible dowel pegs, finger joints and interlocking components that echo traditional Japanese joinery. An elaborate polished teak staircase with a stepped banister snakes around the hall, which has sumptuous Tiffany stained-glass panelled doors. A handmade sanctum of rich materials and even richer craftsmanship, the Gamble House earns its place in the genre known as 'Ultimate Bungalows'. **PC**

Dates: Born 1939   **Nationality:** English   **Location:** St. Austell, Cornwall, England   **Date Completed:** 2000   **Style | Movement:** High Tech

A leading light in the British High Tech movement, Sir Nicholas Grimshaw views his design philosophy as perpetuating the pioneering spirit of the great Victorian architect/engineers. Like his contemporaries Norman Foster and Richard Rogers, he deploys a palette of modern, high-performance materials that permit him to exceed the technical achievements of his nineteenth-century heroes, who include Joseph Paxton and Isambard Kingdom Brunel. His body of work closely mirrors that of these two historic figures, for he has designed both railway stations and botanical gardens. Developed with engineers Anthony Hunt Associates, the dynamic glass and steel vault, 400 m (1,300 ft) long, of his sweeping Eurostar Terminal at London's Waterloo station is a worthy successor to Brunel's work at Paddington and Bristol. Grimshaw's greatest popular success remains the Eden Project, whose interconnected biomes resemble a cluster of soap bubbles, foaming in a former china clay pit. Inspired by Buckminster Fuller's geodesic systems, the structure's hexagonal modules (the largest of which measure 11 m (36 ft) across) act as frames for pneumatic pillows of wonder-polymer ETFE, which are kept inflated to form the necessary insulating layer. An ultra-modern incarnation of Paxton's innovative glass houses, the Eden Project reaffirms Grimshaw's deep ideological roots. **PC**

Gropius Walter

Dates: 1883–1969   **Nationality:** German   **Location:** Dessau, Saxony-Anhalt, Germany   **Date Completed:** 1926   **Style | Movement:** Modernist

A legendary architect and educator, Walter Gropius ranks alongside modernist luminaries Le Corbusier and Ludwig Mies van der Rohe. All three worked as assistants in Peter Behrens' studio, whose design work for industrial giant AEG encompassed everything from graphics and metalware to manufacturing facilities. Though relatively progressive, Behrens did not go far enough for the young Gropius, as illustrated by his first commission after leaving to practise with Adolf Meyer. Where Behrens's AEG Factory was an Egyptian-style temple of industry, Gropius's Fagus Factory (1913) was a lesson in pure, objective design, utilizing a concrete frame to daringly omit corner columns so that the exterior glazing could float between floors. Appointed Director of the State Bauhaus in 1924, Gropius was obliged to use the existing buildings on the Weimar campus, but when politics forced the school to relocate to Dessau in 1925 he seized the chance to issue a new concrete manifesto. Once again, he exploited the reinforced concrete frame, this time to create the floating four-storey glass curtain walls of the school's workshop block, where he strove to unite all the arts under one roof, expanding on even Behrens's diversity of activities. Under Gropius, the Bauhaus at Dessau became the ideas factory that changed the world of design education forever. **PC**

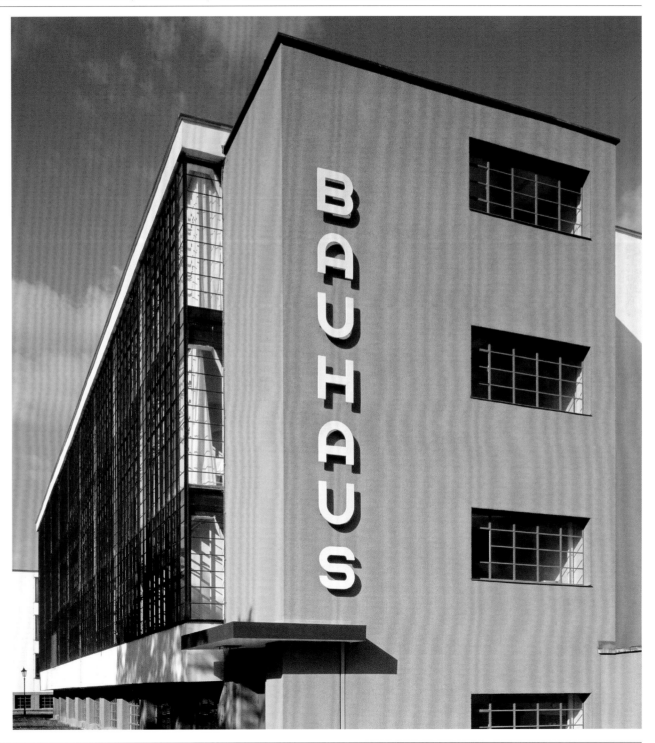

Hadid Zaha

Dates: Born 1950   **Nationality:** Iraqi / British **Building:** Phaeno Science Centre   **Location:** Wolfsburg, Germany   **Date Completed:** 2005   **Style | Movement:** Deconstructivist

It is a tribute to her skill and tenacity that Dame Zaha Hadid has emerged as one of the world's most celebrated architects, with a signature style that attracts iconic commissions. Female, Muslim and Iraqi-born, she stands in stark contrast to her contemporary 'star-chitects', the majority of whom are white, male and Anglo/American. Hadid's work is similarly unconventional: she first became known for complex, idiosyncratic paintings and drawings, creating a distinctive vision that she later transferred to the virtual world of parametric modelling software. The resulting fluid structures morph into the landscape with a plasticity made viable by new material technologies. After a slow start, Hadid's building career followed an exponential curve as she won seven major architectural competitions between 1999 and 2001. Her largest project realized at that date, the Phaeno Science Centre floats 7 m (23 ft) above an undulating park of ramps and craters, on ten immense inverted cones that appear to have been sucked, vortex-like, from the body of the building. These required the largest application of self-compacting concrete in Europe, with a special admixture that sidestepped the impossible task of vibrating the air out of the complex shuttering. After years confined to paper projects, Hadid has cemented her position as one of architecture's most adventurous form makers. **PC**

Hardouin-Mansart Jules

Third phase of the Palace of Versailles

Dates: 1646–1708 **Nationality:** French **Location:** Versailles, France **Date Completed:** 1708 **Style | Movement:** French Baroque

Jules Hardouin-Mansart was the great-nephew of François Mansart, who gave us the mansard roof. The royal architect for King Louis XIV during the second half of his reign, Hardouin-Mansart was the man charged with making real his master's ambitious and extravagant projects. Funding was not an issue. He first worked for Louis on the huge Château de Clagny. Then, in 1678, the king commanded him to more than double the size of the palace at Versailles. He started with the creation of the Galerie des Glaces (Hall of Mirrors) over Le Vau's second-storey rooftop terrace. Then he added two enormous wings to the north and south of the central palace block. In the environs he designed the Orangerie, the Grand Trianon, the horseshoe-shaped stables and a number of royal dwellings. His final project for Versailles was the chapel. In Paris itself, Hardouin-Mansart designed numerous prestige projects—the Pont Royal, the Dôme des Invalides, the Église Saint-Roch, and two huge ceremonial piazzas, the Place des Victoires and the Place Vendôme, both settings for large equestrian statues of the *Roi Soleil*. To complete such a huge workload he ruthlessly deployed a large and capable staff to work out many of the details of his grandiose schemes. **SF**

Hawksmoor Nicholas

St. George's Church

Dates: 1661–1736 **Nationality:** Scottish **Location:** London, England **Date Completed:** 1731 **Style|Movement:** English Baroque

Nicholas Hawksmoor learned his trade as a pupil of Sir Christopher Wren, working on Chelsea Hospital, St Paul's Cathedral, Greenwich Hospital and William and Mary's south front of Hampton Court Palace as well as churches ravaged during the Great Fire of London. He also worked for Sir John Vanbrugh on Blenheim Palace and Castle Howard. A scholar of religious architecture and iconography of all denominations and ages, he made frequent use of obelisks, pyramids and other arcane symbols in his work. The second wave of post-fire church building saw Hawksmoor design six new parish churches in London. He topped the sixth, St George's in Bloomsbury, with a pyramid-shaped pinnacle (influenced by Pliny's description of the tomb of Mausolus at Halicarnassus) capped with a statue of George I dressed as St George in Roman costume, with lions and unicorns gambolling at his feet. The church has seen many changes since its opening: in 1781 the interior was reorientated to a north–south configuration, with windows blanked out when the reredos moved; in the nineteenth century the sculptures on its tower were recarved; in the twentieth it was placed on the buildings-at-risk register. Happily, between 2002 and 2006 nearly £10 million brought St George's back to its former glory. Today, with its east–west axis restored, Hawksmoor would recognize his work once again. **SF**

Heatherwick Thomas

Dates: Born 1970 **Nationality:** English **Location:** Expo 2010, Shanghai, China **Date Completed:** 2010 **Style|Movement:** Contemporary Modernist

Thomas Heatherwick trained as a furniture designer, but his cross-disciplinary career is dotted with pavilions and art installations, which have helped bring him to the public eye. While studying at the Royal College of Art, he was already thinking on a larger scale, spending a summer building a laminated birch gazebo in Sir Terence Conran's garden. Upon graduating in 1994 he founded his own studio, intent on fusing architecture, sculpture, design and engineering in search of creative solutions. His largest commission to date was the prestigious British Pavilion for Expo 2010 in Shanghai. Popularly known as the Seed Cathedral, it took the form of a box, 15 m (50 ft) square and 10 m (33 ft) tall and pierced by 60,000 identical clear acrylic rods in whose inner tips were cast some 250,000 seeds. The rods behaved like fibre optics, drawing in light so that the seeds glowed by day, while creating a hairy halo of light specks at night. Heatherwick topped this artistic coup by designing the Olympic Flame for London 2012, whose kinetic ballet of copper petals uniting to form a single cauldron became an iconic image of the games. Though many of his greatest works have been temporary, Heatherwick's creative flair with form and meaning has left a lasting impression on millions. **PC**

Hernández Agustín

Dates: Born 1924   **Nationality:** Mexican   **Location:** Bosques de las Lomas, Mexico City, Mexico   **Date Completed:** 1990   **Style | Movement:** Contemporary Modernist

During the Renaissance the line between architecture and sculpture was frequently blurred, for talents such as Borromini and Michelangelo regarded each as an extension of the other. This concept of architecture as sculpture persists in some contemporary designs, such as the complex geometric compositions of architect and sculptor Agustín Hernández, whose own home is a striking example of how a house can become more than a dwelling. With little affordable flat land remaining in the richer suburbs, Casa Hernández was designed to exploit a precipitous, 65-degree slope accessed by road along its upper edge. For Hernández, 'symmetry is orderly equilibrium' and though the whole house appears to be in a dramatic state of flux it is actually tethered at its balancing point. The four prisms that comprise the main accommodation are threaded through the 'eyes' of two immense 35 m (115 ft) concrete uprights, supported by massive beams at top and bottom. The lower prisms project out at front and rear, connecting the house to the road behind and forming a panoramic balcony from which to view the city. With their vocabulary of terraced slopes and triangles, Hernández's considered compositions consciously marry modernity with the angular Aztec pyramids of Mexico's pre-Columbian past. **PC**

Herzog Jacques and de Meuron Pierre   National Stadium | The Bird's Nest

Dates: Born 1950 (both)   **Nationality:** Swiss   **Location:** Beijing, China   **Date Completed:** 2008   **Style | Movement:** Contemporary Modern

Born less than a month apart, Jacques Herzog and Pierre de Meuron met while studying architecture at Zurich's Swiss Federal Institute of Technology and, finding they shared similar ambitions, went into practice together in 1978. Their professional partnership has been phenomenally successful with a continuous stream of high-profile commissions and competition wins. The inventive conversion of Bankside Power Station into the popular Tate Modern (2000) brought them to public attention, and contributed to their being jointly awarded the prestigious Pritzker Prize in 2001. The jury's chairman cited their virtuosity for exploring 'the integument (covering) of architecture,' and the pair have consistently experimented with novel exterior finishes, from the polycarbonate facades of the Laban Dance Centre (2003) to the glowing ETFE foil pillows of the Allianz Arena (2005). They also use conventional materials in startling ways and together with their collaborator, contemporary Chinese artist Ai Weiwei, produced the architectural highlight of the 2008 Beijing Olympics. The red-painted inner concrete bowl of the National Stadium is wrapped in a seemingly random basket of silver-painted steel beams, originally intended to disguise the supports for a deleted retractable roof. The arresting aesthetic of 110,000 tonnes of sculpted metal swooping and looping over spectator's heads has led to the stadium's popular moniker, 'The Bird's Nest'. **PC**

Hoffmann Josef Franz Maria

Dates: 1870–1956 **Nationality:** Austrian **Location:** Brussels, Belgium **Date Completed:** 1911 **Style | Movement:** Early Modern / Jugendstil

In the dying years of the nineteenth century, the artists and architects of the Vienna Secession led a stylistic revolution towards a sleeker, more modern and central European interpretation of design. One of the founding members was Josef Hoffmann, an architect, teacher and designer of domestic furniture, fabrics and household items. In time Hoffmann fell out with the Secession and moved on to found the Wiener Werkstätte (Vienna Workshop) in 1903, a collaborative association between architects, designers and clients whose artistic vision was to produce beautiful but functional structures. The following year he designed the Purkersdorf Sanatorium, a luxury spa for wealthy clients. Its success led to a commission from the rich and sophisticated banker and financier Adolphe Stoclet to design a luxurious private mansion. For its time, the Palais Stoclet is a stark, almost forbidding, modernist cuboid structure, clad in white Norwegian marble, with distinct foreshadowings of Art Deco style. The building has a stair tower to one side, embellished with four figures sculpted by Franz Metzner, and a prominent entrance loggia. The interior is designed by artists from the Wiener Werkstätte and shows distinct Jugendstil tendencies, the highlight of which are Gustav Klimt's stunning decorative mosaic wall panels in the principal rooms. **SF**

Holden Charles Henry

Dates: 1875–1960   **Nationality:** English   **Location:** London, England   **Date Completed:** 1932   **Style|Movement:** Modernist

Beacons of progress in a suburban sea of mock-Tudor homes, Charles Holden's stations for London Underground offered many their first experience of modernism. Ironically, Holden rejected the modernist tag, regarding his solutions simply as appropriate design. He had begun his career designing in historically inspired styles, from Arts and Crafts to Tudor Revival, but his work always displayed clean lines, restrained detailing and tightly sculpted forms. He grew ever more austere as he worked on

the Imperial War Graves Commission on the World War I cemeteries in France, and when he began designing his first Underground stations in 1923, he produced restrained white Portland stone facades that carefully incorporated the vivid red and blue signage. Before designing the Piccadilly Line extension in 1930, Holden embarked upon a tour of northern Europe with the company's general manager, Frank Pick, to observe developments in modern architecture. He incorporated his findings into a

series of brick, glass and concrete stations that were to define the network's image. His personal favourite was the great light-filled rotunda of Arnos Grove's ticket hall whose cylindrical form had been inspired by Gunnar Asplund's monumental Stockholm Public Library (1928). With its air of elegant simplicity and efficiency, Arnos Grove represents Holden's own successful journey towards modernity. **PC**

Holl Steven

Dates: Born 1947   **Nationality:** American   **Location:** Amsterdam, Netherlands   **Date Completed:** 2000   **Style | Movement:** Modern

New York-based Steven Holl is known for sensuous buildings that consciously use light as an extra dimension as well as for his phenomenological approach, in which the sensory properties of building materials are as important as the character of their environment. Consequently his ultra-modern buildings harmoniously inhabit their various urban or rural locations. When Steven Holl Architects was asked to convert the old Sarphatistraat Federal Medical Supply Warehouse in Amsterdam into offices, it was an apparently unremarkable project. But after renovating the four-storey U-shaped brick building, Holl attached a spongy-looking rectangular building within the complex but facing onto the Singelgracht Canal. Clad with three-dimensionally perforated copper—which has oxidized into pale, rippling greens—Holl's building is also an optical construction that plays with shapes and colours, especially at night when the shifting lights are reflected in the waters of the canal. The perforated copper is a subtle reference to the mathematical concept of the Menger Sponge, which encloses no volume but displays an infinite surface area. Additionally, the building is inscribed with a concept from *Patterns in a Chromatic Field*, a musical piece from Morton Feldman. Inside it holds a public meeting space and staff restaurant. **SF**

Hollein Hans

Haas-Haus

Dates: Born 1934 **Nationality:** Austrian **Location:** Vienna, Austria **Date Completed:** 1990 **Style|Movement:** Postmodernist

There are many layers to Hans Hollein's Pritzker Prize-winning career, including architect, industrial designer, civil engineer and lecturer. Graduating in 1956 with an engineering degree in Vienna, Hollein gained a fellowship to continue his education in the United States. His graduate studies in architecture and planning at Chicago's Illinois Institute of Technology were followed by a master's degree in architecture from the prestigious University of California in Berkeley. Despite having studied and worked under legendary modernists Ludwig Mies van der Rohe and Richard Neutra, Hollein was to become a vocal critic of Functionalism and the concept that a facade should exist only to serve a practical purpose. He made his stance clear with the highly controversial Haas-Haus, a retail and restaurant development facing St Stephen's Cathedral in a sensitive conservation area of Vienna. The structure rises on a retail arcade, before jutting out like a medieval timber building to meet a curved glass facade, to which a veneer of stone elements has been partially added forming the window frames. Together with the prominent projecting rotunda, this glazing offers up a mirror to the neighbouring cathedral's spires, as though reminding the viewer that most modern city buildings stand layered upon the ruins of their medieval forbears. **PC**

Hopkins Michael

Sir Harry and Lady Djanogly Learning Resource Centre

Dates: Born 1935 **Nationality:** English **Location:** Jubilee Campus, University of Nottingham, Nottingham, England **Date Completed:** 1998 **Style | Movement:** Contemporary Modern

Sir Michael Hopkins, in collaboration with his wife Patricia, works through his London-based practice Hopkins Architects. Their design philosophy is to use traditionally crafted materials, such as wood and stone, in combination with contemporary engineering, to achieve energy-efficient, chic modern buildings. Their signature works are light-weight steel and glass compositions, but they have also pioneered the use of permanent fabric structures, most notably with the Mound Stand at Lord's

Cricket Ground and the Lawn Tennis Association's National Tennis Centre at Roehampton, both in London. Their other notable works include the hugely successful London 2012 Velodrome for the Olympics and Portcullis House on the Embankment. For the University of Nottingham Hopkins designed the first phase of the Jubilee Campus using an artificial lake as its focal point. The most striking building is the Djanogly Learning Resource Centre, situated on an island platform in the middle of the

campus lake. Intriguingly, this library building has only a single floor that winds its way upward and outward around the circumference of the building. The resulting building cantilevers steeply out from its base like a huge fruit bowl. Designed to be as environmentally friendly as possible, it has solar panels and grass-covered roofs. **SF**

Horta Victor

Dates: 1861–1947   **Nationality:** Belgian   **Location:** Brussels, Belgium   **Date Completed:** 1901   **Style | Movement:** Art Nouveau

Victor Horta, the pioneer of Art Nouveau, is best known for the works he created during a critically acclaimed decade designing elegant homes for wealthy Belgians, most notably his four great Brussels town houses. One of these is Maison Horta, the mansion and studio he built for himself: today it is the Musée Horta. These grand homes are celebrated not just for their design, but also for the essential link they provide in the history of architecture between the classical tradition and the modern movement. The exterior of Maison Horta has an elegant stone facade complemented by delicate iron balcony railings; the interior open-plan layout was revolutionary. A vast glass ceiling floods the principal staircase with light, which pours into the building, illuminating the graceful curves and exuberance of the Art Nouveau forms. Horta, however, eventually found himself bored with the style and changed to a more restrained and forward-looking approach, abandoning the organic, sinuous shapes and forms of Art Nouveau in favour of designs based on geometric patterns, which more easily accommodated the latest advances in building technology. This is the style in which he designed the reinforced-concrete Palais des Beaux-Arts (1928) in Brussels, foreshadowing the arrival of Art Deco. **SF**

Isozaki Arata

Dates: Born 1931 **Nationality:** Japanese **Location:** Los Angeles, CA, United States **Date Completed:** 1986 **Style | Movement:** Postmodern

Arata Isozaki was first identified with Metabolism, a Japanese architectural movement of the late 1950s that aimed to build flexible cities that could respond organically to the demands of modern society, expanding and changing as required. Isozaki has gone on to author major projects around the world, particularly in Japan and Western Europe. His work defies easy labelling because he refuses to employ a signature style, personalizing each of his projects by synthesizing the social, political and cultural elements unique to that commission. This often results in the fusion of Eastern ideas into Western projects. In his first building in the United States, MOCA Grand Avenue, this quest took on a specifically geometric form as Isozaki sought to find an homage to both the Western idea of the golden section and the Eastern philosophy of yin and yang. Half of this low, rough-textured, red-sandstone building complex is a museum; the rest comprises shops, apartments and a hotel, separated by a terraced courtyard. A dramatic semi-cylindrical roof brings light and space to the administrative section; glazed pyramids of varying size light other parts of the building. The galleries are all subterranean and lead into each other from left to right. Built at a cost of £14 million (around £30 million today), and providing 2,300 m² (24,500 sq ft) of exhibition space, the building is seen as the finest example of Isozaki's later work. **SF**

Ito Toyo

Dates: Born 1941 **Nationality:** Japanese **Location:** Kensington Gardens, Hyde Park, London, England **Date Completed:** 2002 **Style | Movement:** Contemporary Modern

A persistent theme in Toyo Ito's architecture is his exploration of the ephemeral character of Japanese cities, and the transient nature of their structures. Unlike Western metropolises, which typically have dense brick and concrete dwellings and fixed reference points, Japan's urban centres are in a constant state of flux, with buildings frequently demolished and replaced within just 20 years. Even twentieth-century Japanese cities were largely timber-built for ease of reconstruction following frequent earthquakes, and the iconography of trees features heavily in Ito's work. The commission to design the third annual Serpentine Pavilion was the perfect vehicle for his vision of nomadic urban culture, which he expresses in temporal, dematerializing structures without clearly defined boundaries. Working with engineer Cecil Balmond, the complex intersecting geometry of the design was derived mathematically from an algorithm of a cube that gradually expanded as it was rotated.

Extensive use of glass between white steel elements helped reduce the visual mass of the composition, and the irregular openings across walls and ceiling hinted at an abstract forest canopy. Though Ito's later works, such as the Tod's Omotesando Building (2004), assume a more concrete permanence, he keeps returning to the organic forms of intersecting branches framing floating, flush-mounted glass. **PC**

Jacobsen Arne

Dates: 1902–71   **Nationality:** Danish   **Location:** Oxford, Oxfordshire, England   **Date Completed:** 1963   **Style | Movement:** Scandinavian Modern

A Dane with a passion for detail, Arne Jacobsen excelled at every scale, from a coffee pot to an Oxford college. Initially apprenticed to a mason, he won an architectural scholarship to the Royal Danish Academy of Fine Arts in 1924 and then a silver medal for a chair design at the great 1925 Paris Exposition Internationale des Arts Décoratifs. Furniture became integral to Jacobsen's reputation, particularly abroad, and he designed several classic chairs, including the best-selling, three-legged

Ant (Model No. 31000). His Swan and Egg chairs were created specifically for the SAS Royal Hotel in Copenhagen, which he designed in its entirety, from tower to ashtrays. It was after staying at this hotel in 1958 that Oxford University awarded Jacobsen the commission for St Catherine's College, and he delivered a thoroughly contemporary quad of modernist buildings and interiors. So great was his desire to control all aspects of the campus that he added a clause to his contract that allowed him to

lay out the gardens and design the internal fixings. This he duly did, going so far as to specify chub and Golden Orf fish for the ponds. Now Grade I listed, St Catherine's encapsulates Jacobsen's life-long obsession with integrated detail and proportion. **PC**

Jahn Helmut

Dates: Born 1940   **Nationality:** German / American   **Location:** Berlin, Germany   **Date Completed:** 2000   **Style|Movement:** Contemporary Modern

The eighth member of the Chicago Seven (architects who rebelled against the dominant modernist narrative of the mid-1970s, and who named themselves after a notorious group of radical anti-war activists), Helmut Jahn has become one of the most successful international architects of modern times. His company, Murphy/Jahn Architects, specializes in prestige projects such as the Messeturm of the Frankfurt fair grounds, the European Union Headquarters in Brussels and Suvarnabhumi Airport in Bangkok. Jahn has said that his aim is to take everything away from a building until he is only left with the necessary parts. Initially a modernist, over time Jahn has embraced 'creative rationalism', an approach to design that he sees as more flexible than the formality of modernism, and he is credited with paving the way for a new era of sustainable buildings. For the 26-floor Bahn Tower (Sony Centre) in Berlin, Jahn created a sleek, curve-fronted tower of glass, which encloses a light-filled urban forum. Both the roof and the facades filter and moderate the light, providing a constantly altering and refracting effect that changes throughout the day and night. Designed for cultural and social interaction at ground level, the higher levels of the building contain offices and work spaces. **SF**

Jefferson Thomas

Dates: 1743–1826   **Nationality:** American   **Location:** Charlottesville, VA, United States   **Date Completed:** 1809, frequently remodelled until 1826   **Style | Movement:** Palladian

The principal author of the Declaration of Independence, the third president of the United States was a true polymath. Architecture was but one of his many accomplishments. Self-taught, Thomas Jefferson based his work on observations and enquiries made during his extensive travels abroad and also from books, in particular Andrea Palladio's *Four Books of Architecture*, which he used as a primer. The result was a personal synthesis of classic architectural styles embracing Roman,

Renaissance, French and English ideas. He said, 'Architecture is my delight and putting up and pulling down one of my favourite amusements.' He started with a loathing of his native Virginian architecture and vowed to improve it, eventually becoming America's first truly great native-born architect. By the time he died Jefferson left a number of notable buildings, mostly in neo-Roman style, including the Virginia State Capitol, the University of Virginia buildings, and two villas for himself, Poplar

Forest (his private home) and Monticello (his public house). He also contributed to the city plan of Washington, DC. Jefferson's masterpiece, however, is Monticello, designed in classic Palladian style. He was constantly improving it—parts were pulled down and rebuilt six or seven times—calling it his 'architectural laboratory,' and the building was unfinished when he died there in 1826. **SF**

Jensen-Klint Peder Vilhelm

Grundtvigskirken | Grundtvig's Church

Dates: 1853–1930 **Nationality:** Danish **Location:** Copenhagen, Denmark **Date Completed:** 1940 **Style | Movement:** Expressionist

Peder Jensen-Klint first trained as an artist, then later qualified as a building engineer when he found himself drawn to architecture. Inspired by early Danish vernacular buildings, his first works were small, experimental, red-brick villas. He was so successful that the Danish Architects Association admitted him as a member even though he had no formal training. Then Jensen-Klint won an architectural competition with a bold brick Danish Expressionist-style building for a memorial church for the Danish philosopher and social reformer, N.F.S. Grundtvig. Construction on Grundtvigskirken started in Copenhagen in 1921. On completion the front elevation soared in a jagged silhouette of stepped gables, almost 50 m (164 ft) high. The nearly six million pale yellow bricks were set in place by seven carefully selected master masons. Jensen-Klint died after the main tower was completed, nine years into the project. His son, Kaare Klint, took over the supervision until 1930 and his grandson, Ebsen Klint, eventually finalized the building. Grundtvigskirken's cavernous interior comprises a nave, two lateral aisles and a small transept, supported by towering columns and ribbed vaulting which give the stark interior a memorable grandeur and elegance. It is the largest Evangelical Lutheran church in Scandinavia. **SF**

Jiřičná Eva

Joseph Store

Dates: Born 1939   **Nationality:** Czech   **Location:** 26 Sloane Street, London, England   **Date Completed:** 1989   **Style | Movement:** High Tech

Having left her native Czechoslovakia following the Prague Spring of 1968, architect/engineer Eva Jiřičná was to start her own small revolution in London's retail environment. After a year at the Greater London Council and a decade working on the Brighton Marina she moved to the Richard Rogers Partnership, leading the interior design of the steely Lloyd's Building. Leaving Rogers in 1982, Jiřičná successfully collaborated with a number of architects, including fellow Czech, Jan Kaplický, with whom she designed the influential Way In store for Harrods. This success led to her founding her own practice and designing a series of minimal high-end shops for the entrepreneurial fashion designer, Joseph Ettedgui. Bringing an architectural approach to interior design, Jiřičná solved the Sloane store's poor circulation with a showpiece staircase that betrayed her engineering training. Constructed from an exquisite web of steel rods and cables meeting in polished, precision junctions, the transparent glass treads of each stair appear to float weightlessly in mid-air allowing light to flood down into the store. Jiřičná's signature staircases have become ever more complex and daring, with commissions from private individuals, and public institutions (including the Victoria & Albert Museum's Jewellery Gallery), but she will always be remembered as the architect who brought High Tech to the high street. **PC**

Johnson Philip

AT&T Building | now Sony Building

Dates: 1906–2005 **Nationality:** American **Location:** New York City, NY, United States **Date Completed:** 1984 **Style | Movement:** Post-Modernist

In one of architecture's sharpest ironies, the man who introduced modernism to the American mainstream would undermine its ethos by designing the country's first great postmodern monument. Gifted a family fortune while still a student at Harvard University, the wealthy Philip Johnson took frequent tours of Europe where he befriended architect Ludwig Mies van der Rohe and encountered the work of the nascent modernist movement. Johnson showcased his 'discoveries' at New York's Museum of Modern Art in 1932, co-curating the highly influential 'Modern Architecture – International Exhibition'. Having aided Mies's emigration to the United States in 1937, Johnson decided to retrain as an architect himself, building his own famous Glass House in 1949, which has many visual parallels with the Farnsworth House, begun by Mies in 1946. Johnson's long career saw him designing many corporate and cultural buildings that moved steadily away from the modernist ideal, culminating in the controversial headquarters for communications giant, AT&T. Johnson chose to cap his 37-storey tower with an immense open pediment seemingly borrowed from an antique Chippendale wardrobe, representing a flat rejection of the controlled functionality of modernism. For a man so full of contradiction, it is difficult to know if the AT&T was a sincere gesture, or simply a prank call. **PC**

Dates: 1573–1652 **Nationality:** English **Location:** Greenwich, England **Date Completed:** 1635 **Style|Movement:** Palladian

After being inspired by Andrea Palladio's work on his travels to Italy, Inigo Jones became the first real star of English architecture. He rose to prominence working for Anne of Denmark, the wife of King James I, devising costumes and sets for court masques. The first building Jones is known to have designed is the New Exchange in the Strand, London, for the Earl of Salisbury in 1608. By 1614 he was Surveyor of the Kings' Works and had the job of building a royal hunting lodge at Greenwich for the queen. Appropriately known as the Queen's House, due to her untimely death in 1616 it was not completed until 1635. Although built on a difficult site on either side of a public road leading to Deptford—Jones built a covered bridge between the two sections—the building was a masterpiece of Palladian architecture and hugely influential. Today's building is much modified. The road has gone; Charles II added rooms over the bridge and colonnades were added in the nineteenth century. Elsewhere Jones designed the new Banqueting House in the Palace at Whitehall and the first London square at Covent Garden, with the accompanying Palladio-inspired church of St Paul. He died in 1652 in Somerset House, one of his greatest buildings. **SF**

Juvarra Filippo

Dates: 1678–1736 **Nationality:** Italian / Sicilian **Location:** Turin, Italy **Date Completed:** 1731 **Style | Movement:** Baroque

The Sicilian Baroque architect Filippo Juvarra earned a living as a set designer for opera, theatre and elaborate public festivities before making his name as an architect. His only building in Rome, the Antamoro chapel in San Girolamo della Carità, is a Baroque explosion featuring a dramatically backlit statue of St Filippo Neri by Pierre Le Gros. Six years later, in 1714, Victor Amadeus II of Savoy (soon to be King of Sicily) engaged Juvarra to design the Basilica di Superga, a church, mausoleum and monastery on a high hill overlooking Turin. Victor Amadeus had vowed to do so in 1706, when he and Prince Eugene of Savoy planned the relief of beseiged Turin from the top of the 670 m (2,200 ft) mountain. Victory the next day liberated the city and saw the withdrawl of Louis XIV's Franco-Spanish troops from north Italy. The task was not straightforward: first the hilltop had to be flattened and lowered by 40 m (130 ft), which took two years, then all the building materials had to be lugged to the top. It took over 14 years of toil in total, but the result was a triumph. The basilica is surmounted by a huge dome over a high drum and flanked by two symmetrical campanile. Much of the building was built from stone quarried from the foot of the hill and marble from the best quarries in Italy. Juvarra was nine months into grandiose plans for the rebuilding of the Alcázar in Madrid when he died. **SF**

Kadri Iftikhar M.

Dates: Born 1930   **Nationality:** Indian   **Location:** Delhi, India   **Date Completed:** 1986   **Style|Movement:** Modernist

After a childhood in Ahmedabad and university in Pune, Iftikhar Kadri moved to Mumbai. Established in 1960, Kadri's architectural practice has seen stellar growth since those early days. With new blood in the form of Iftikhar's son, Rahul, and today with regional offices in Bangalore and Oman, Kadri brought modern architecture to India with a string of industrial townships, commercial properties, hospitals and other large projects. These include a number of hotels, such as the Breach Candy Hotel in Mumbai, the conversion of Lake Palace in Udaipur into the 'most romantic hotel in India', the Taj Coromandel in Chennai, and the Dubai Ramada, which boasts a vast stained-glass mural made by John Lawson. At 41 m (135 ft) high and 9 m (30 ft) wide, this was listed in the *Guinness Book of Records* as the tallest stained-glass structure in the world. The Nehru Centre was devised to promote the teachings and ideals of Pandit Jawaharlal Nehru, the first prime minister of independent India. The complex includes a planetarium, theatre, art galleries, research centres and the Discovery of India building, named after Nehru's great book of the history of India, written during his imprisonment at Ahmednagar. **SF**

Kahn Louis

The National Assembly Building of Bangladesh

Dates: 1901–74   **Nationality:** American   **Location:** Capital complex, Dhaka, Bangladesh   **Date Completed:** 1983   **Style | Movement:** Modernist

An influential professor at the universities of Yale and Pennsylvania, Louis Kahn's name remains revered within the architectural world for the distinctive style he developed in his fifties. Kahn sensed something missing in the repetitive, mechanical character of post-war modernism, and found the qualities he sought touring the ancient ruins of Greece and Rome in the 1950s. For Kahn, these possessed the moving spirituality and monumental grandeur that modernism lacked, and he evolved a highly personal vocabulary of elemental forms in concrete, brick and stone, whose monumentality was countered by the play of natural light within them. The last of the commissions that made his reputation, the National Assembly Building of Bangladesh is composed of a central circular assembly chamber, ringed by cylindrical and cuboid forms, each housing a distinct state function. Massed like a medieval citadel with massive geometric windows, their facades are built from plain grey concrete veined with rich white marble that emphasizes the layered construction. Sadly, Kahn never saw his masterpiece completed, suffering a fatal heart attack in a restroom at New York's Pennsylvania station while returning from Bangladesh. With the address crossed out in his passport, it took police several days to identify him, for he left them with only his name. **PC**

Kaplický Jan

Dates: 1937–2009 **Nationality:** Czech **Location:** Lord's Cricket Ground, London, England **Date Completed:** 1999 **Style | Movement:** Biomorphic

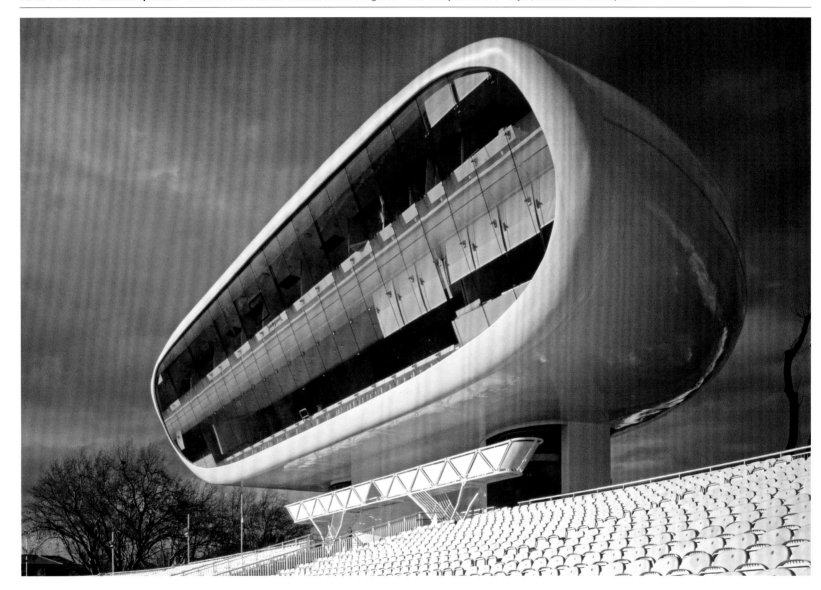

The son of a sculptor and a botanical illustrator, Czech émigré Jan Kaplický combined sensuous, organic forms with cutting-edge technology to create a highly original body of work. After escaping to London following the 1968 Prague Spring, Kaplický worked for a succession of High Tech architects, including Foster, Rogers and Piano, but found creative freedom in evenings spent sketching curvaceous alternatives to their cuboid structures. In 1979 Kaplický set up a think-tank called Future

Systems with David Nixon, producing detailed hand-drawn cross-sections of nomadic living capsules. Raised on robotic arms or air-lifted by helicopter, their aeronautical forms related to space-race themes of survival and exploration. Amanda Levete joined Future Systems in 1989 after Nixon had left for America, and she married Kaplický two years later. The couple's first major commission was the soaring new media centre for Lord's Cricket Ground: an elliptical semi-monocoque structure whose

smooth aluminium skin hides a forest of welded ribs and beams. It was constructed by a Dutch shipbuilder, then ferried to London in sections to be welded together on site. The practice went on to complete the biomorphic landmark of Selfridges in Birmingham (2003) but the Media Centre still best encapsulates the spirit of the man who thought outside the box. **PC**

Kellogg Kendrick Bangs

High Desert House

Dates: Born 1934   **Nationality:** American   **Location:** Joshua Tree, CA, United States   **Date Completed:** 2003   **Style | Movement:** Organic

Kendrick Bangs Kellogg believes in integrating architecture with its natural environment and, since receiving his architect's licence in 1964, has specialized in private residences for wealthy patrons desiring bespoke surroundings. The High Desert House was created for the successful watercolour artist Bev Doolittle, whose widely collected work revolves around nature, animals and Native Americans. She often combines them with her 'camouflage technique', where the faces of animals and Indians are hidden within a natural landscape. Her house followed a similar conceit, with Kellogg leaving the boulder-strewn site intact and incorporating the existing topography into his designs. The roof is composed of 26 overlapping concrete leaves, morphing out of concrete trunks rooted on separate boulders. These 'trees' are designed to sway gently in the event of seismic activity, while their thermal mass provides both insulation and radiant heating. Citing a brief 1955 meeting with Frank Lloyd Wright as his inspiration, Kellogg's architecture is organic in every sense, from its biomorphic forms and skeletal structures to its flowing plans and fluid connections to their context. Even the act of building assumes a natural evolution with decisions constantly made with craftsmen on site. His buildings grow through the slow accretion of concrete, copper and steel, layered like sedimentary rock. **PC**

Kim Swoo Geun

Dates: 1931–86   **Nationality:** Korean   **Location:** Seoul, South Korea   **Date Completed:** 1984   **Style | Movement:** Contemporary modern

Kim Swoo Geun is considered to be the father of modern Korean architecture and, appropriately enough, has likened his buildings to a philosophical womb: 'The womb's home is the mother, the mother's home is the house and the house's home is the environment.' When introducing modern architecture to Korea, he made the change acceptable to his countrymen by incorporating local ideas concerning the environment and space, resulting in buildings that naturally flow like traditional Korean architecture. To realize his ideas he founded, in 1960, what became the architectural SPACE Group, which led to the launch of Korea's first major arts and architecture magazine *Space*, in 1966, and the Space Group Building, in the 1970s. Kim designed more than 70 buildings across Korea—such as the Freedom Centre in Seoul, the Kyungdong Presbyterian Church and the Jinju National Musem—but he is best known internationally for his work on the main sports stadium in Seoul. Sitting beside the Hangang River, it was commissioned for the Tenth Asian Games and then used again for the 1988 Summer Olympics. Kim took the profile of an elegant Korean Joseon Dynasty porcelain vase as his inspiration for the shape of the stadium. For the Olympics, the exterior was hung with a vast art installation featuring colourful recycled plastic bottles while the interior provided covered seating for 100,000 spectators. **SF**

Klerk Michel de

Dates: 1884–1923 **Nationality:** Dutch **Location:** Amsterdam, Netherlands **Date Completed:** 1920 **Style | Movement:** Expressionist

One of the founding members of the Amsterdam School, Michel de Klerk was recognized as an outstanding and original talent while still a youth. Unfortunately, very few of his designs have been built. De Klerk designed in Expressionist style, using brickwork to great effect to create imposing buildings of strength and character; he also designed furniture and interiors. De Klerk's first job was a housing block at Vermeerplein; he then moved on to contribute designs for the Scheepvaarthuis (Shipping House), which was completed in 1916. Between 1913 and 1921 de Klerk designed three distinctive, stylistically similar housing association blocks for the dockers and railway workers of the Spaarndammerbuurt district in Amsterdam. The third building, known as Het Schip (The Ship), is his masterpiece. Rich in detailed design, it contains 102 homes for workers as well as a school, a meeting hall and a post office at the 'prow'. Nautically inspired, the red-brick building appears to ripple due to the horizontal bands of brick and tile, which indicate the varying floor levels. At the northern end of the block an ornamental brick pinnacle is purely visual. The blocks are regarded as supreme examples of the Amsterdam School. **SF**

Knobelsdorff Georg Wenzeslaus von

Dates: 1699–1753   **Nationality:** Prussian   **Location:** Potsdam, Germany   **Date Completed:** 1747   **Style | Movement:** Rococo

A Prussian soldier, Georg Wenzeslaus von Knobelsdorff's love of painting influenced his decision to resign his commission in 1729, becoming a self-taught gentleman architect, studying—as so many of his contemporaries—by travelling first to Italy and then France. These trips were financed by his friend the Crown Prince, later Friedrich Wilhelm II of Prussia. On his return he was made responsible for the royal residences. The king praised his picturesque style and they frequently discussed city planning and architecture together. Knobelsdorff's first project—in collaboration with Johann Gottfried Kemmeter—was to enlarge and improve Rheinsberg Palace near Berlin. His first significant building was the lavish Berlin Opera House, designed in English Palladian style. Then, in collaboration with Frederick, he redesigned the Tiergarten hunting grounds in Berlin into a public park and royal gardens; Knobelsdorff received particular praise for turning the drainage ditches into pretty waterfalls. Frederick desired a summer palace in Potsdam and handed over his sketches to Knobelsdorff to realize. The result was much more intimate than Versailles, a one-storey rococo palace surrounded by a terraced vineyard, reflecting the ideal of harmony between humans and nature. However, disagreements between king and architect soured their relationship and Jan Bouman, rather than Knobelsdorff, finished the palace. **SF**

Dates: 1925–2004   **Nationality:** American   **Location:** Los Angeles, CA, United States   **Date Completed:** 1958   **Style | Movement:** Southern California Modern

Pierre Koenig was a pioneer of energy-efficient buildings, using solar heating and passive cooling systems for his hot climate homes. Koenig refuted ornamentation as excessive and financially extravagant, utilizing industrial technology in tandem with steel as his primary structural element and devising buildings that expressed simple architectural and material truths. Koenig devised his own language of architecture, but his style has since come to epitomize southern California. He first expressed these stripped-down formal ideas in the small glass-and-steel-framed house that he built for himself in 1950. He went on to use his small houses as prototypes for considerably larger projects by repeating the elements. By using stand-ard structural parts he used the economy of mass production to keep building costs to a minimum. Encouraged by John Entenza's Case Study House Programme, set up in 1945 to provide modern answers to an anticipated post-war housing boom, Koenig used industrial techniques to produce a simple one-storey steel-framed villa with a flat roof, his Case Study House No. 21. The north and south elevations are completely glazed while the east and west facing walls are solid. The house is surrounded by pools of water; in hot weather, the water can be hydraulically pumped onto the roof and then can cascade down through scuppers and back into the pools to cool the air. **SF**

Koolhaas Rem

Dates: Born 1944   **Nationality:** Dutch   **Location:** Seattle, WA, United States   **Date Completed:** 2004   **Style | Movement:** Deconstructivist

Pritzker Prize-winning architect and theorist Rem Koolhaas has achieved that rare feat of being as successful in practice as in print. Having begun his career as a screenwriter and journalist, Koolhaas enrolled at London's Architectural Association (AA) in 1968 before taking up a research fellowship in New York, where he would write the book that launched his career. *Delirious New York: A retroactive manifesto for Manhattan* (1978) was Koolhaas's critique of the city's evolution and architecture,

and was quickly hailed as a classic text. One of its recurring themes was interrogation of the 'program', which Koolhaas defined as the process of deliberately editing the function of a building and the behaviour of its occupants. Koolhaas co-founded the Office for Metropolitan Architecture (OMA) in 1975 with colleagues from the AA and it continues to generate consistently unconventional buildings as vehicles for exploring his theories. Combining his dual preoccupations of publishing and 'program,'

the Seattle Public Library is an 11-storey envelope of glass and steel. Its faceted form is driven by the 'programs' within, for the exterior folds to follow the irregular stacked floor plates that differ in size according to their intended activities. As happy editing buildings as books, Koolhaas is an architect whose work demands a little background reading.
PC

Kuhne Eric

Dates: Born 1951 **Nationality:** American **Location:** Queen's Island, Belfast, Northern Ireland **Date Completed:** 2012 **Style|Movement:** Contemporary Modern

By the latter half of the twentieth century, many architects were becoming disenchanted with the cold sterility of modernism, viewing its clinical purge of ornament as effectively a robbery, depriving buildings of cultural nuance. A vocal advocate for 'the storytelling qualities of architecture,' Eric Kuhne has spent the last 30 years exploring ways to restore this vital property by reintegrating architecture, landscape and interior design to create great civic spaces with stories to tell. Educated at Rice University where he majored in both art and architecture, Kuhne opened his own practice while still studying for his masters at Princeton, where he also worked in the office of leading postmodernist Michael Graves. Kuhne relocated to the United Kingdom in 1994 to mastermind the design of Kent's Bluewater shopping centre. Loaded with pertinent local references, from a sculpted frieze of London's Guilds to rooftop ventilators modelled on Kentish oast houses, it remains the largest and most successful retail destination in Europe. His most recent work is the gleaming Titanic Belfast, which opened in time to commemorate the centenary of the *Titanic*'s maiden voyage. Carefully evolved through studies of crystals, icebergs, ships' hulls and the White Star Line's logo, it successfully tells its embedded stories through its faceted form and finish. **PC**

Kurokawa Kisho

Nakagin Capsule Tower

Dates: 1934–2007   **Nationality:** Japanese   **Location:** Tokyo, Japan   **Date Completed:** 1972   **Style|Movement:** Metabolist

Kisho Kurokawa was one of the founders of the Japanese Metabolist Movement in the late 1950s and early 1960s, which took avant-garde style and merged it with traditional elements. These included the very Japanese concept of impermanence, with the result that Metabolist projects usually contained elements that could be removed, adapted, renewed and interchanged when required. Kurokawa was deeply concerned with sustainable and eco-friendly buildings and took to politics to promote his ideas. He used modern technologies and materials in his buildings alongside a distinctly Japanese aesthetic. He liked to use open steel frames and prefabricated units for maximum flexibility of design and considered the city to be a dynamic entity that should easily adapt to the needs of its citizens. For the 14-storey Nakagin Capsule Tower, Kurokawa exposed all the utilities: lift shaft, pipework, ducts and the capsules themselves, all of which are clearly visible on the exterior.

Nothing was politely hidden and nothing artificially coloured; all elements were true to the nature of their materials. The tower holds 140 capsules, each offset around a central core, and each held in place by four bolts: all detachable and replaceable. Every capsule has a circular window and was pre-assembled with a built-in bed and bathroom unit, all sized for one person. **SF**

Labrouste Pierre-François-Henri Reading Room of Bibliothèque Sainte Geneviève

Dates: 1801–75 **Nationality:** French **Location:** Paris, France **Date Completed:** 1850 **Style | Movement:** Italian Renaissance Revival

Classically trained, Henri Labrouste was both an architect and an engineer who became the leading exponent of cast-iron construction. He believed that 'form must always be appropriate to function … a logical and expressive decoration must derive from the construction itself'. Among his first projects were a controversial restoration of the Graeco-Roman temples at Paestum in Italy in 1828, an asylum at Lausanne, Switzerland and a prison in Alessandria, Italy. Labrouste firmly believed that

architecture should reflect society, and put this into practice in his first big commission, the reading room of the Bibliothèque Ste-Geneviève in the fifth *arrondissement* of Paris, in 1839. He produced a long two-storey building in Romantic-Classicist style with a roof supported by 15 slender cast-iron Ionic columns that support the roof independently of the masonry walls. The columns also divide the interior into twin barrel-vaulted spaces, which are formed from pierced-leaf-pattern cast-iron arches and

constructed from iron-mesh wires hidden under the plaster. The reading room fills the entire first floor and is flooded with light from the surrounding high windows. It was the first time that high technology was introduced into a monumental building. With this success behind him, Labrouste was asked to design a reading room for the Bibliothèque Nationale in Paris—he produced a similar design but on a much bigger scale. **SF**

Langhans Carl Gotthard

Dates: 1732–1808   **Nationality:** Prussian   **Location:** Berlin, Germany   **Date Completed:** 1791   **Style | Movement:** Neoclassical

Carl Gotthard Langhans was an untrained architect yet managed to design one of the most iconic buildings in Germany—the Brandenburg Gate. He was well educated in the law, mathematics and languages, and had a particular passion for the antique texts of Vitruvius. Langhans first worked for the German royal family in 1766 when he was called in to help on Castle Rheinsberg. For the next few years he was sent—at Friedrich Wilhelm II of Prussia's expense—to study the buildings of Italy, France, England, Belgium and the Netherlands. In 1788 Langhans, now Court Superintendent of Buildings, was commissioned to rebuild the old Brandenburg Gate, the monumental entrance to Unter den Linden that leads up to the residence of the Prussian monarchs. Given the theme of peace, Langhans devised a monumental neoclassical design based on the Propylaea gateway to the Acropolis in Athens. Consisting of six Doric columns on either side, the gateway provides five portals with the widest central passageway originally reserved for royalty. Designed by Johann Gottfried Schadow, the Quadriga of Victory bringing peace to Berlin, rides on top of the gateway and dates to 1793. **SF**

Larsen Henning

The Ministry for Foreign Affairs

Dates: Born 1925   **Nationality:** Danish   **Location:** Riyadh, Saudi Arabia   **Date Completed:** 1984   **Style | Movement:** Regional Modernist

One conundrum facing many emerging states is how to devise their own architectural identity when most prototypes for modern buildings originate in the Western world. Seeking ways to embrace modernity while respecting their own traditions, the Saudi government held a competition in 1979 to design the Ministry of Foreign Affairs. It was won by Danish architect Henning Larsen, who had previously worked for the legendary modernist Arne Jacobsen. His concept was an ingenious fusion

of cultures, blending modest Arabian vernacular with Scandinavian modernism as well as suggestions of the Moorish Alhambra. The triangular plan followed the age-old model of Arabian domestic architecture, which presents an austere, blank face to the outside world while reserving its richness for the privacy of internal courtyards. The ministry's low silhouette and thick walls derive from the squat adobe fortresses of the Nedj, the plateau at the heart of Saudi Arabia, but this defensive,

sun-baked exterior gives way to wonderfully cool internal streets, which are lit by shafts of natural light from circular skylights high in its vaulted ceilings. Referencing Arabia's old bazaars, it provides a comfortable and secure means of circulation between the offices and amenities, and presents a successful synthesis of Muslim and modernist design. **PC**

Lasdun Denys

Dates: 1914–2001   **Nationality:** English   **Location:** London, England   **Date Completed:** 1976   **Style | Movement:** Brutalist

Le Corbusier, Maxwell Fry and Berthold Lubetkin were primary influences for Sir Denys Lasdun, who infused their social commitment and modernist principles into his architecture. One of his early projects was the Hallfield Estate scheme and accompanying primary school, both built using reinforced concrete. Next were four 14-storey apartment buildings in Bethnal Green, linked together by a central lift tower and stair block to encourage a community feeling. In the late 1950s he inserted a simple slab of

modernist flats between two classical buildings in St James's Place; this was his first example of 'strata', in which geometric buildings are ultimately inspired by natural geological forms. In 1963, as Denys Lasdun & Partners, he was commissioned to design a new National Theatre complex on the South Bank of the Thames. This required three theatres, bars, restaurants, theatre offices and workshops, all of which he made out of reinforced concrete, formed into an urban landscape of interlocking terraces;

he likened the project to designing a small city. The complex was roundly criticized but Lasdun replied that he and 'strata' had given the Thames back to London. However, his favourite building remained his work for the Royal College of Physicians, one of the few post-war buildings to be Grade I listed, next to Nash's Regency buildings edging Regent's Park in London. **SF**

Latrobe Benjamin Henry

The White House

Dates: 1764–1820 **Nationality:** American **Location:** Washington, DC, United States **Date Completed:** 1829 (North Portico); numerous subsequent renovations **Style | Movement:** Neoclassical

Benjamin Henry Latrobe, the 'father of American Architecture', was born, bred and trained in Great Britain before starting private practice in 1791. After his wife's death in 1795 he emigrated to the United States, where he was the first fully trained architect. He was working in Virginia when his Greek Revival design was chosen for the Bank of Pennsylvania and he moved to Philadelphia, where his practice flourished. In 1801, his friend Thomas Jefferson involved him in expanding the White House, to which they added colonnades. After the British Army burnt down the White House in 1814, the original architect, James Hoban, rebuilt it, and later added porticoes of a similar style to those proposed by Latrobe. By that time Latrobe was concentrating his efforts on restoring the Capitol after its similar fate. In 1803 Jefferson had made him surveyor of the Public Buildings of the United States and hired him to oversee construction of the Capitol. He was responsible for building the south wing and, after this was finished in 1807, started work on the north. After the fire he worked exclusively on the Capitol until 1817, producing the fine neoclassical interiors that can still be seen in the National Statuary Hall, the Old Senate Chamber and Old Supreme Court. **SF**

Lautner John

Dates: 1911–94 **Nationality:** American **Location:** Los Angeles, CA, United States **Date Completed:** 1960 **Style|Movement:** Modernist

A hands-on architect, John Lautner executed daring designs that bear the can-do attitude of an American pioneer. At the age of 12, Lautner began helping his father build a summer cabin on the shores of Lake Superior, hauling timber and laying floors. His predilection for practical problem-solving was also in evidence at Frank Lloyd Wright's Taliesin Fellowship, where he preferred carpentry and plumbing chores to the drawing studio. Helping to build Taliesin West with his own hands, he developed the material knowledge to back up his bold ideas and, upon leaving Taliesin in 1938, he set up practice in Los Angeles, where he was to design the string of houses that made his name. Amongst the most-filmed of these iconic structures is the Chemosphere, whose outwardly futuristic aesthetic conceals a frame of laminated timber beams. Designed for aerospace engineer Leonard Malin, this octagonal flying saucer perches on an 8 m (26 ft)-tall concrete pillar, which is rooted in an otherwise unbuildable 45 degree sloping site. Discrete underside vents allow air to be drawn up through double-skinned walls, then circulated inside the house before being expelled through the roof's apex. A floating wooden house that functions like a jet engine, the Chemosphere remains one of Lautner's most inventively engineered solutions. **PC**

Le Corbusier (Charles-Edouard Jeanneret-Gris)   Notre-Dame-du-Haut Chapel

Dates: 1887–1965   **Nationality:** Swiss   **Location:** Ronchamp, France   **Date Completed:** 1955   **Style | Movement:** Modernist

It would be hard to overstate Le Corbusier's importance in the development of modern architecture. Decades after his death, his work remains a universal point of reference for architects, who define themselves through opposition or accord. Ironically, the great man's work was to end in opposition to itself. A brilliant self-publicist, Le Corbusier brought his brand of pure, functional modernism to the world, only to abandon it in favour of wilful, anti-rational forms. The hard, white box of his Villa Savoye (1931) was the physical incarnation of his famous 'Five Points of Architecture': raised off the ground on slender *piloti*, designed to an open plan, with a free facade, long horizontal windows and a flat roof garden, it contained all the components of a 'machine for living'. The chapel he completed at Ronchamp 24 years later stands in stark contrast, with a sail-like concrete roof, inspired by a shell, that billows above a coarse-rendered mass of curving walls, punched with small oblong windows. Despite the roof's visible mass, it seems to float lightly, a few centimetres above the walls, on barely visible columns. Often cited as the most influential building of the twentieth century, the outwardly contradictory Ronchamp only enhanced Le Corbusier's long-term reputation. After all, the rules were his to break. **PC**

Legorreta Vilchis Ricardo

Fashion and Textile Museum

Dates: 1931–2011 **Nationality:** Mexican **Location:** London, England **Date Completed:** 2003 **Style | Movement:** Regional Modernism

In his own words, 'walls, water and earth colours, the three elements from Mexican culture,' sum up the work of Ricardo Legorreta Vilchis, who also used light and open spaces to produce modern designs that were rooted in the traditions of his homeland. Protégé of the Mexican modernist architect Luis Barragán, Legorreta studied under José Villagrán, first at university and then for ten years with Villagrán's firm before starting his own company in 1964. He designed prolifically, creating a remarkable collection of both residential projects and the public work that gave him worldwide prominence, such as the pink-and-yellow-fronted Camino Real hotel in Mexico City, Pershing Square in Los Angeles, with its ten-storey purple bell tower, San Antonio's red Central Library, and the striking pink and ochre exterior of the Fashion and Textile Museum in London. This converted warehouse was redesigned by Legorreta to the commission of British fashion designer Zandra Rhodes, who saw one of his house designs in Los Angeles. The colourful result—'like finding a cockatiel nestling among the sparrows'—is all the more arresting thanks to its street location. In 1999 Legorreta became the sixth person to receive the International Union of Architects Gold Medal; the next year he received the Gold Medal of the American Institute of Architects; and in 2011 Japan's Praemium Imperiale. **SF**

Libeskind Daniel

Jewish Museum

Dates: Born 1946 **Nationality:** Polish / American **Location:** Berlin, Germany **Date Completed:** 1999 **Style|Movement:** Deconstructivist

The child of Holocaust survivors, Daniel Libeskind left Poland for the United States in 1959. An accomplished musician and set designer, he gained his professional architecture degree in 1970, but it was not until 1989, the year he founded Studio Daniel Libeskind with his wife, Nina, that his first major commission came, for the Jewish Museum in Berlin. The result was a remarkable tour de force: an unsettling, Deconstructivist building clad in titanium-covered zinc, which follows a jagged, irregular floorplan. In Libeskind's view, 'Architecture is not based on concrete and steel and the elements of the soil. It is based on wonder.' The Jewish Museum, with its dramatic entrance and underground passages, the brutal slashes of its windows and the stark Holocaust Void that runs within it, certainly fulfils this brief. Since its completion, Libeskind has designed projects all over the world, from the Imperial War Museum North in Manchester—a shattered globe torn apart by conflict—to Reflections at Keppel Bay, a waterfront development in Singapore involving leaning towers topped with sculptural lattices. Work progresses on his most complex project to date, the reworking of the site of the destroyed twin towers in New York, for which he won the competition to produce the architectural masterplan: he had experienced the original construction at first hand while a student at Cooper Union. **SF**

LOOS Adolf

Dates: 1870–1933   **Nationality:** Austro-Hungarian / Czech   **Location:** Prague, Czech Republic   **Date Completed:** 1930   **Style | Movement:** Early Modernist

Architecture has often inspired impassioned debate, but few style critiques have been as scathing as 'Ornament and Crime'. Published in 1908, Adolf Loos's famous essay was a venomous denouncement of the flowing, wilful forms of Art Nouveau and specifically the Vienna Secession, which was then the height of bourgeois fashion. Issuing a searing call to strip ornament from architecture, (with no pretence of what, today, we might call political correctness), Loos wrote that, because the majority of the prison population had tattoos, such decoration must mark its owners as either 'latent criminals or degenerate aristocrats'. Such assertions bolstered Loos's argument that the application of ever-more elaborate ornamentation hastens the pace at which an object or building goes out of fashion and is deemed obsolete. Following his mantra of eliminating ornament from useful objects, he designed a series of increasingly pared-back private houses, which are now considered pioneering works of modernism. Outwardly austere, their interiors employed rich materials such as marble, but even these were applied in simple planes to create 'smooth and precious surfaces,' intended to have a timeless quality. Villa Müller was the last house he designed and its plain-white rendered exterior punched with unadorned windows proves Loos remained a man of his word. **PC**

Lubetkin Berthold

Penguin Pool

Dates: 1901–90   **Nationality:** Russian   **Location:** London Zoo, London, England   **Date Completed:** 1934   **Style|Movement:** Modernist

It might have frustrated Berthold Lubetkin to learn that his best-remembered work is a pool for penguins, rather than progressive homes for people. Born in remote Georgia, Lubetkin moved to Moscow on the eve of the Russian Revolution, and was inspired by radical Constructivist designers, in particular their concept of architecture and technology as potential tools for social change. He extended his education in Berlin, Warsaw and Paris, where he met Le Corbusier and studied concrete construction under Auguste Perret. Lubetkin's first commission was a set for a circus performers' nightclub, Club Trapèze Volant (1927). He moved to London in 1931, formed the architectural group Tecton with a clutch of young graduates from the Architectural Association, and gained a series of commissions from London Zoo. The second of these was the penguin pool, which had spiralling white cantilevered ramps that allowed its inhabitants to parade before their viewing public. It was engineered by the talented Dane, Ove Arup, who cleverly concealed the substantial supporting abutments of the ramps within the nesting boxes. Though he would later design projects like the showcase social housing development at Spa Green (1950) it was the pirouetting ramps of the penguin pool that best encapsulated Lubetkin's Constructivist ideals of the 'artist engineer.' **PC**

Dates: 1869–1944 **Nationality:** English **Location:** Sulhampstead, Berkshire, England **Date Completed:** 1912 **Style | Movement:** Arts & Crafts

Though lacking any formal education until he entered the South Kensington School of Art at the age of 16, Sir Edwin Lutyens rapidly rose to become the pre-eminent architect of his generation. Designer of both London's respectful Whitehall Cenotaph (1920) and New Delhi's regal Viceroy's House (1931), his name is as synonymous with the architecture of the British Empire as Kipling's is with its poetry and prose. Yet Lutyens's most enduring legacy lies with his domestic work, which helped define the popular rural English idyll. Kept away from school by rheumatic fever, the young Lutyens spent much of his time visiting the local Tickner's builder's yard in Godalming, where he developed a keen knowledge of both traditional materials and construction techniques. Much influenced by the great Arts and Crafts architects Philip Webb and Norman Shaw, Lutyens combined his builder's knowledge with a flair for spatial design, producing outwardly conservative houses with highly inventive plans. Folly Farm is a fine example of his considered craftsmanship, with its rich red brick walls, long sloping tiled roofs and weather-boarded gable ends, overlooking a naturalistic country garden designed by his long-time collaborator, Gertrude Jekyll. Solid, warm and comforting, Lutyens's great houses have a style that will remain forever England. **PC**

Mackintosh Charles Rennie

Dates: 1868–1928   **Nationality:** Scottish   **Location:** Helensburgh, Scotland   **Date Completed:** 1903   **Style | Movement:** Arts & Crafts / Art Nouveau

After an apprenticeship with John Hutchison, from whom he learned draughting, in 1889 Charles Rennie Mackintosh joined the recently formed Honeyman & Keppie partnership. While there, he continued to take classes at the Glasgow School of Art, where he met Margaret MacDonald, who would become his wife in 1900 as well as his major collaborator. He won a number of prizes for his work, culminating in 1890 with a design for a neo-Greek public hall that won him the £60 Alexander Thomson Travelling Studentship. He travelled in Italy and returned to become the lead designer at Honeyman & Keppie. Mackintosh's designs from this period include the Glasgow Herald Building (1895). Today it is called The Lighthouse, and it houses Scotland's Centre for Design and Architecture. In 1897, Mackintosh won the competition to build the new Glasgow School of Art on a new site in Renfrew Street, and the result was a masterpiece. In 1903—a partner of the firm since John Honeyman's retirement in 1901—he produced his domestic triumph, high above the River Clyde. Hill House, designed for the Glasgow publisher Walter Blackie, is a synthesis of all Mackintosh's influences: Arts and Crafts, Art Nouveau, Scottish Baronial and Japonisme. Together, he and Margaret also designed much of the interior and the furniture. **SF**

Mather Rick

Dates: Born 1937   **Nationality:** American   **Location:** Keble College, University of Oxford, Oxford, England   **Date Completed:** 1995   **Style | Movement:** Contemporary Modern

An American architect from Portland, Oregon, Rick Mather came to England in 1963 to study urban planning at the Architectural Association. He decided to stay and practise in London, and it is with a pleasing irony that this talented guest from overseas has made the reinvigoration of great British institutions his speciality. Notable examples include his airy Neptune Court at the National Maritime Museum (1999), the sensitive extension of Soane's Dulwich Picture Gallery (2000) and the light-filled courtyard for the Wallace Collection (2000). A fine example of Mather's context sensitivity is the new accommodation block for yet another British bastion. The ARCO Building at Keble College, Oxford, shares a quad with the flamboyant polychrome brickwork ranges, designed by the exuberant William Butterfield in 1870. Choosing one colour from Butterfield's loaded palette, Mather clad his block in beautiful handmade Welsh bricks, but differentiated old from new by using vertical soldier courses, honestly expressive of the fact these bricks bear no load. Special corner bricks, which are square in cross-section, allow these ranks of soldiers to march around the facades without breaking step. Dedicated to the fine detail, Mather remains a worthy reminder that cultural sensitivity is not the sole preserve of native architects. **PC**

Mayne Thom

Dates: Born 1944 **Nationality:** American **Location:** Los Angeles, CA, United States **Date Completed:** 2005 **Style | Movement:** High Tech

Thom Mayne, who co-founded the southern Californian design group Morphosis, designs buildings that have non-traditional forms, but which display a deep understanding of the culture in which they are located. Commissioned for a California Department of Transportation headquarters in downtown Los Angeles, Mayne produced a modern, environmentally friendly and distinctly futuristic design that has become an urban landmark. The 13-storey Caltrans District 7 Headquarters sits over an underground car park and fronts a large public plaza and an accessible, ground-floor public lobby; it announces itself with a 12 m (40 ft)-high, forward-canted sign reading '100' (the number of its South Main Street address) in super-graphics. The north facade appears to be windowless but is in fact made from perforated aluminium panels in front of a double skin of glass; these panels open and close automatically, triggered by the sun's angle and intensity. This provides a kinetic skin with constantly varying configurations across its surface, which protects office workers from strong sunlight and provides them with changing views. The third floor has a unique glass-floored conference room. Between the fourth and 13th floors, the southern facade is covered with photovoltaic cells, which generate around five per cent of the building's energy requirements. **SF**

McAslan John

Dates: Born 1954   **Nationality:** Scottish   **Location:** London, England   **Date Completed:** 2012   **Style|Movement:** Modernist (redevelopment of Victorian original)

John McAslan is one of Britain's leading architects, and his practice has been responsible for the design of a plethora of significant buildings worldwide. In particular, McAslan has proved remarkably successful in the regeneration and restoration of older buildings, such as the De La Warr Pavilion on Britain's south coast, the Stanislavsky Factory and Theatre site in Moscow and the Iron Market at Port-au-Prince, Haiti, which was devastated by both a 2008

fire and a 2010 earthquake. These buildings were given new life by enhancing the original designs with modern additions, a strategy also evident in the work done on Lewis Cubitt's King's Cross station. The centrepiece of the £547-million redevelopment is an ambitious semicircular concourse that spans the entire length of the station, built in the 1850s. The engineering company Arup, structural designers of the Sydney Opera House, provided the diagrid

system, supported by a funnel and sixteen 'tree' columns—all in white steel—that ensured no load was placed on the Victorian structure. This allowed McAslan to open up the 150 m (500 ft) western facade for the first time since 1972, and to show it off with Europe's largest single-span station structure, seen here from the balcony on the opposite side of the concourse. **SF**

Mehmed Ağa

Sultan Ahmed Mosque | The Blue Mosque

Dates: c. 1540–c. 1617   **Nationality:** probably Albanian   **Location:** Istanbul, Turkey   **Date Completed:** 1617   **Style | Movement:** Late Classical Ottoman

Sedefkâr Mehmed (Ağa is an honorific) learnt his trade from the master of classical Islamic architecture, Mimar Sinan, and became chief imperial architect in 1606. 'Sedefkâr' means a worker in mother-of-pearl, and Mehmed literally made this name for himself by working in nacre before becoming Sinan's assistant. An example of his handiwork is the throne now in the Topkapı Palace museum, which he made for Ahmed I. He continued to use mother-of-pearl ornamentation in Sultan Ahmed Mosque, in locations such as the marble minbar, the pulpit where the Imam gives his sermon. The sultan's tomb is incorporated on the northwest corner of this complex, which includes six minarets, a madrasa, shops, a Turkish bath, a hospital, fountains and a kitchen for the poor as well as the sultan's own prayer chamber. Built over the Byzantine hippodrome and imperial palace, the mosque took eight years to construct and both architect and sultan died before the complex was finished. Standing opposite Hagia Sophia, the pinnacle of Byzantine church architecture, the mosque—nicknamed the Blue Mosque by visitors after the mainly blue Iznik tilework—was designed to surpass its predecessor, mirroring the domes of the earlier building with a cascade of its own. The result is a breathtaking high point of Islamic architecture. This photo looks over the madrasa (domes in foreground) and the sultan's mausoleum (dome closest to photographer). **SF**

Meier Richard

Dates: Born 1934   **Nationality:** American   **Location:** Los Angeles, CA, United States   **Date Completed:** 1997   **Style | Movement:** Modernist / Rationalist

With his singular pursuit of architectural purity, Richard Meier has kept the spirit of early modernism alive in his careful compositions of pristine white forms. After graduating from Cornell University in 1957, Meier travelled to Europe, where he sought out Le Corbusier's early work from the 1920s. Shortly after returning to the United States, he found employment with former Bauhaus tutor Marcel Breuer, who provided Meier with another direct link to pioneering modernism. Having established his own practice in 1963, Meier came to international attention through the book *Five Architects* (1972), which documented his early modernist-inspired works alongside those of Peter Eisenman, Michael Graves, Charles Gwathmey and John Hejduk. Labelled 'The New York Five' or 'The Whites', they were involved in a public confrontation with five anti-modernist architects (dubbed 'The Grays'), aligned with influential postmodernist Robert Venturi. Undeterred, Meier has stayed true to his colour, his style climaxing in the monumental Getty Center. Rising above Los Angeles like an American Acropolis, this £800 million complex of museums, galleries and research facilities combines modernist curves with monumental masonry. Set against walls of textured travertine blocks, the flowing contours of Meier's smooth white-painted steel panels continue to fly the early modern flag. **PC**

Melnikov Konstantin

Dates: 1890–1974   **Nationality:** Russian   **Location:** Moscow, Russia   **Date Completed:** 1931   **Style | Movement:** Constructivist

Konstantin Melnikov, born to a poor family, had a lucky break when he met Vladimir M. Chaplin, an engineer who supported him through 12 years of study at the Moscow School of Painting, Sculpture and Architecture. Melnikov's early work was neoclassical, but in the early 1920s he embraced the avant-garde, attracting critical approval for his Soviet Pavilion at the 1925 Paris Expo, after which his patron Chaplin wrote to him: 'I'm happy that I was lucky to notice a sacred flame in a slim little boy.' Between 1927 and 1929 he enjoyed his 'golden season' when he designed and built six workmen's clubs, one in Likino-Dulyovo and five in Moscow. He also built for himself, on 10 Krivoarbatsky Lane in Moscow, a stunning house made from two interlocking cylinders with no load-bearing walls and nearly 60 hexagonal windows—38 of them in the workshop on the third floor. Barry Bergdoll has called it 'one of the most important house designs of 1920s modernism'. After falling out with the Soviet authorities, from 1937 he was denied the opportunity to practise architecture. Apart from a few competition entries in the 1950s and 1960s, he did not work again. Today, his legacy is under threat. The land his house stands on is valued at more than £25 million, making it a target for developers in a city where money talks. **SF**

Mendelsohn Erich

Dates: 1887–1953   **Nationality:** German   **Location:** Potsdam, Germany   **Date Completed:** 1921   **Style|Movement:** Expressionist

It is said that Albert Einstein, after being shown round Erich Mendelsohn's unique building, pronounced it 'organic', a cryptic verdict that could have been either praise or criticism. The tower was designed to accommodate an unmovable telescope, which had been constructed to record red shift—an effect predicted in Einstein's Theory of Relativity—and an underground laboratory. Originally planned in reinforced concrete, post-World War I restrictions as well as difficulties inherent to the medium meant that much of the visible building was made of brick and covered in plaster. Nevertheless, the tower was influential and quickly attracted a host of visitors. In 1924, along with Mies van der Rohe and Walter Gropius, Mendelsohn was one of the founders of the 'Ring of Ten' in Berlin, an architectural collective founded to promote the 'new architecture' and later expanded to include other German and Austrian architects. Fleeing Nazi anti-Semitism in 1933, Mendelsohn went first to England where he worked in partnership with Serge Chermayeff, designing the De La Warr Pavilion in Bexhill-on-Sea, East Sussex, and planning a number of projects in Palestine. From 1941 he worked in the United States, settling finally in San Francisco. His first commission in the US was the B'hai Amoona Synagogue in University City, Missouri—the first of a number of synagogues and buildings for Jewish communities. **SF**

Mengoni Giuseppe

Dates: 1829–77   **Nationality:** Italian   **Location:** Milan, Italy   **Date Completed:** 1877   **Style | Movement:** Neoclassical

Milan is an international fashion centre known for its retail opportunities: nowhere is that more obvious than in *il salotto di Milano* (Milan's living room), as the galleria is nicknamed. Connecting the piazzas of the cathedral and La Scala opera house, the galleria is a landmark in the development of retail architecture and one of the oldest shopping malls in the world. Prada and Louis Vuitton ply their trade at the central crossing point under the great iron and glass octagon designed by Bolognese architect Giuseppe Mengoni, who won the 1860 competition to redevelop the area. The foundation stone was laid on March 7, 1865, by the first king of unified Italy, Vittorio Emanuele II of the House of Savoy, whose coat of arms is represented in a colourful patriotic mosaic, as are those of the cities of Rome, Florence, Milan and Turin. Today, above the mosaics, just below the 39 m (128 ft)-diameter dome, are four huge frescos depicting the continents of Africa, America, Asia and Europe. Two years later, in 1867, the partially completed galleria was opened to the public and was an immediate success. In spite of this, money was always a problem for Mengoni, who ended up funding the monumental triumphal arch on the Piazza del Duomo. Ironically, Mengoni died in a fall from scaffolding two days before the king opened the galleria.
SF

Mies van der Rohe Ludwig   Barcelona Pavilion | a.k.a. German Pavilion

Dates: 1886–1969   **Nationality:** German / American   **Location:** Barcelona, Spain   **Date Completed:** 1929 (reconstructed 1986)   **Style | Movement:** Modernist

One of the twentieth century's great architect-educators, Ludwig Mies van der Rohe attained lasting fame for his ubiquitous 'less is more' maxim. From simple beginnings in his father's stonemason's shop, he progressed through the offices of proto-modernists Bruno Paul and Paul Behrens before establishing his own practice designing restrained neoclassical houses. Following World War I, Mies gradually stripped his designs to their bare essentials, culminating in the iconic Barcelona Pavilion at the 1929 International Exposition. Kept deliberately empty to emphasize the purity of its form, the pavilion's thin roof plate appeared to float upon chromed cruciform steel columns, while vertical planes of precious marble, onyx and travertine acted as spatial dividers. Finding few commissions following the Wall Street Crash, Mies became the director of the Bauhaus in 1930, only for it to be closed by the National Socialists in 1933. Emigrating to America four years later, he settled in Chicago and became the influential Head of Architecture at the nascent Illinois Institute of Technology, defining the look of corporate American architecture for decades. His pioneering work was not forgotten in the Old World, and the decision in 1983 to recon-struct his temporary Barcelona Pavilion on its original site would suggest that less is moreish. **PC**

Miralles Moya Enric

Dates: 1955–2000 **Nationality:** Spanish **Location:** Holyrood, Edinburgh, Scotland **Date Completed:** 2004 **Style | Movement:** Post-Modern

Spain was just emerging from Franco's long dictatorship when the young Enric Miralles completed his architectural training in 1978. The return to democracy gave Spanish architecture a boost and the next decade saw Miralles's highly original style attract many commissions, from organic steel pergolas to poetic concrete cemeteries. A consistent thread within his expressive work was the relationship between building and context, with free-form structures responding to the site. Political independence and freedom of expression were pertinent themes to bring to the 1998 competition to design a new Scottish Parliament. Miralles won over the judging panel with his concept for a contemporary Greek agora—an ancient place for public gatherings in support of the democratic ideal. Producing a handful of leaves and stalks, Miralles proceeded to arrange them into an organic diagram of a building that would flow out of the landscape. The final form of the glazed skylight canopies still retains the lines of those folded leaves, while echoes of the stalks can be found everywhere from microphone stands to window grills. Tragically neither Miralles nor the competition's instigator, Donald Dewar, saw the building finished, both suffering fatal brain haemorrhages in 2000. Completed under his wife's supervision, the new Scottish Parliament stands today as Miralles's posthumous masterpiece. **PC**

Moneo Vallés José Rafael — Cathedral of Our Lady of the Angels

Dates: Born 1937   **Nationality:** Spanish   **Location:** Los Angeles, CA, United States   **Date Completed:** 2002   **Style|Movement:** Contemporary Modern

A leading avant-garde architect and winner of the Pritzker Prize (1996), Rafael Moneo is the first Josep Lluis Sert Professor of Architecture at Harvard University. His work is controversial—his annexe to the City Hall of Murcia in the Plaza del Cardenal Belluga has many detractors—but there is no doubt that the Cathedral of Our Lady of the Angels is inspirational. Built at a cost of $163 million to replace the Cathedral of Saint Vibiana, which was damaged in the 1994 earthquake, the new cathedral—the first built in the United States for many years—is the third largest in the world, with a 5,400 m² (58,000 sq ft) nave that seats 3,000, a carillon wall of 36 bells facing the street, 12,000 panes of translucent alabaster, and a series of tapestries by Californian artist John Nava called the 'Communion of Saints', depicting 136 holy people. The cathedral doors do not open straight onto the street. To reach them, visitors have to go through two plazas, and up a grand staircase. The huge 25-tonne bronze doors cost $3 million, and were created by sculptor Robert Graham, as was the Virgin Mary statue, visible above the entrance in the photograph. Designed to withstand a future shock, the cathedral is built on 198 base isolators, designed to float up to 70 cm (27 in) during an earthquake. **SF**

Murcutt Glenn

Dates: Born 1936 **Nationality:** Australian **Location:** Glenorie, Sydney, Australia **Date Completed:** 1983 **Style | Movement:** Modern

One-time disciple of Mies van der Rohe, Glenn Murcutt's approach has changed over the years. Today the motto of Australia's most famous architect is the Aboriginal proverb 'touch the earth lightly,' and his works are designed to fit into the Australian landscape. He does so without the cast of thousands that so many other big-name architects employ— as was pointed out by the Pritzker Prize jury, who summed him up thusly when he won in 2002: 'He is an innovative architectural technician who is capable of turning his sensitivity to the environment and to locality into forthright, totally honest, non-showy works of art.' His primary architectural focus has always been residential, but he has designed public buildings— the Pritzker Prize jury remarking in particular on the Arthur and Yvonne Boyd Education Centre. Murcutt has won a multitude of Australian and international awards, including the Order of Australia and the 2009 American Institute of Architects Gold Medal. He set up in practice in 1969 and soon made a name for himself with his residential work. The single-storey Ball-Eastaway House was built for a pair of artists on the outskirts of Sydney. The house is made of steel, with a wooden floor and a corrugated curved roof. It sits on six columns over a sandstone plateau, thereby allowing water to pass underneath the house without interruption—touching the earth lightly indeed. **SF**

Nash John

Dates: 1752–1835 **Nationality:** English **Location:** Brighton, England **Date Completed:** 1822 **Style | Movement:** Mogul Indian

John Nash trained with Sir Robert Taylor and set up independently in 1777. His early years ended in divorce and bankruptcy in 1783 when he left London for Wales. His work there—and his partnership with Humphrey Repton—saw his star rise again, so much so that from 1810 until 1830 Nash worked under the patronage of the Prince Regent (from 1820, King George IV). During this period he created some of London's iconic vistas, including Regent Street, Carlton House and Cumberland Terrace, Regent's Park and the Regent's Canal, All Souls Church in Langham Place, the Theatre Royal, Buckingham Palace and Marble Arch. Perhaps his best-known work is a more whimsical creation in the centre of what became Londoners' favourite seaside resort. In 1815 Nash was called in to remodel Henry Holland's Marine Pavilion in Brighton to provide 'Prinny' with a magnificent establishment. He did so with a flight of fancy— an Indian-inspired exterior complete with onion domes, pinnacles and minarets, and an extravagant chinoiserie interior. The resulting palace looks more suitable for an oriental potentate than the Prince of Wales. The romantic vision was supported by the cutting-edge technology of the time: gas lighting, a fully plumbed bathroom and flushing water closets. **SF**

Neutra Richard

Dates: 1892–1970 **Nationality:** Austrian / American **Location:** Palm Springs, CA, United States **Date Completed:** 1946 **Style|Movement:** Modernist

After serving in the Austrian cavalry during World War I, Richard Neutra worked for Erich Mendelsohn in Berlin for two years, before emigrating to the United States in 1923. There he set up with Rudolf Schindler, a friend from university, before starting his own practice. He soon made a name with the 'Health House', built for Dr P.M. Lovell in 1929. It was the first steel-framed house in America, an early example of the use of spray-on concrete,

and one of the buildings chosen by MoMA in 1932 to exemplify the 'International Style'. Over the next 20 years he worked primarily on residential properties, which were 'practical, not pretentious'. The Kaufmann House in Palm Springs, which had to sustain temperatures over 37°C (100°F), needed practicality. Neutra designed a radiant heating system that allowed water for the pool to be chilled or heated, and to defend against wind-blown

sand he provided vertical movable aluminium louvres. In 1949, he appeared on the cover of *Time* magazine, and in 1955—now working with Robert E. Alexander—he was one of the small number of top architects employed by the US State Department to design new embassies; his was in Karachi. Neutra returned to Europe in 1966, living and working in Vienna. **SF**

Niemeyer Oscar

Dates: 1907–2012 **Nationality:** Brazilian **Location:** Plaza of the Three Powers, Brasília, Brazil **Date Completed:** 1958 **Style|Movement:** Regional Modernism

Invented in Europe, then exported around the world, modernism tended to morph when exposed to different cultures and climates. It experienced a tropical transformation at the hands of Oscar Niemeyer, whose monumental, abstract concrete forms hint at Brazil's historic love of Baroque architecture. Like many Brazilian architects, Niemeyer was deeply influenced by the work of Le Corbusier, who visited Brazil in 1936 and consulted on the design of the new Ministry of Education and Health in Rio. The young Niemeyer worked on the ministry under Lucio Costa, who subsequently won the 1957 competition to masterplan the new centralized federal capital city. Thanks to his connections with Costa and President Juscelino Kubitschek, Niemeyer was appointed director of public works, proceeding to populate this utopian city, named Brasília, with his own unique creations. Though retaining elements of functional modernism, Niemeyer adored the sensuous curves found on 'the body of the beloved woman' and the Congress is dominated by the concrete dome of the Senate chamber and the upturned bowl of the Chamber of Deputies. Though forced into exile during Brazil's long military dictatorship, Niemeyer later returned to his native land where his work is now so venerated that Brasília has been awarded UNESCO World Heritage Site status. **PC**

Nouvel Jean

Dates: Born 1945   **Nationality:** French   **Location:** Paris, France   **Date Completed:** 1987   **Style | Movement:** High Tech / Contemporary Modern

Educated at the École des Beaux-Arts in Paris, Jean Nouvel achieved world-wide fame with his 1981 competition-winning design for the Institut du Monde Arabe. Jointly founded by the governments of France and 18 Arab nations, the institute's mission is to promote greater Western understanding of Arabian culture through joint research and the dissemination of ideas. Nouvel's concept cleverly combined these themes of transparency and openness with direct references to traditional Arabian architecture realized with contemporary technology. Containing a library, auditorium and exhibition spaces, the institute's most iconic aspect is the southern facade, which reinterprets the delicate wooden *mashrabiya* of Arabia as a kinetic screen of glass and steel. Set behind the glass facade is a geometric grid of over 240 squares, each incorporating 57 photosensitive oculars. Electronically controlled, these open and close like camera apertures, in response to changing light conditions, moderating the internal temperature and glare. This fusion of modern technology with Muslim detail secured Nouvel the 1989 Aga Khan Award for Architecture. He continues to experiment with complex means of modulating light and solar gain—most recently with his Torre Agbar in Barcelona (2005), whose 56,619 transparent and translucent plate-glass louvres tilt at different angles to deflect direct sun rays. **PC**

Dates: 1867–1908   **Nationality:** Austrian   **Location:** Vienna, Austria   **Date Completed:** 1898   **Style|Movement:** Jugendstil (Art Nouveau)

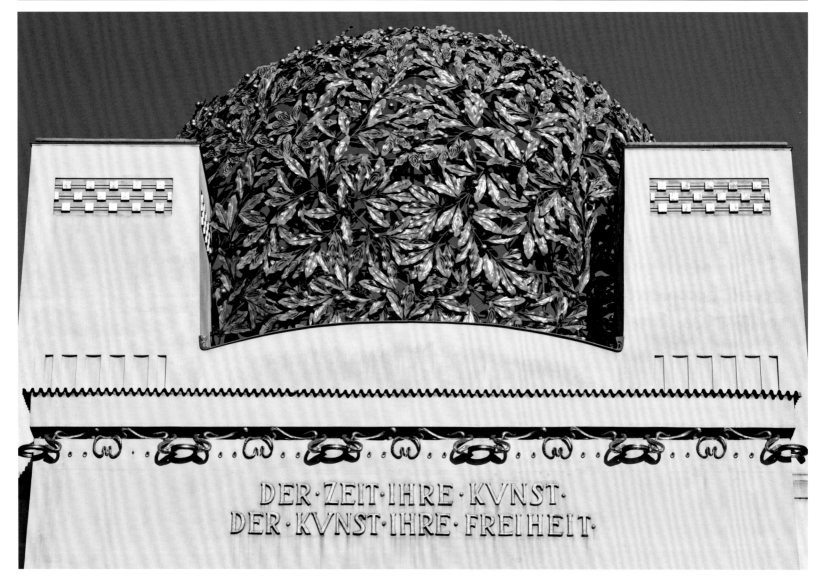

Joseph Maria Olbrich won prizes at the Vienna Academy of Fine Arts, but it was a time of revolution against the art establishment and in 1897 he, along with many others, including fellow architect Joseph Hoffmann and artist Gustav Klimt, resigned from the Association of Austrian Artists, founding the Vienna Secession. Their motto: *Der Zeit ihre Kunst. Der Kunst ihre Freiheit* (To every age its art, to art its freedom). They were joined by Otto Wagner, a prominent professor and architect in whose practice Olbrich worked—together they had been responsible for the Karlsplatz Stadtbahn Station, a brilliant example of Jugendstil. Olbrich was chosen to design an exhibition building, the landmark Secession Hall. The Municipal Council granted permission for a temporary pavilion with a ten-year lifespan: six months later construction was complete, and over a century later the hall is still there. Since the 14th Vienna Secessionist exhibition in 1902, it has housed Klimt's famous *Beethoven Frieze*. After its completion, Olbrich designed the Hochzeitsturm (Wedding Tower) in Darmstadt, another centre of Jugendstil. He also contributed to the Louisiana Exhibition in St Louis and became a corresponding member of the American Institute of Architects, probably at the instigation of Frank Lloyd Wright. Sadly, Olbrich died young from leukaemia. **SF**

Östberg Ragnar

Dates: 1866–1945   **Nationality:** Swedish   **Location:** Stockholm, Sweden   **Date Completed:** 1923   **Style | Movement:** National Romantic / Arts and Crafts

Many late nineteenth-century architects were preoccupied with expressing national identity through design as a counter to the grim, anonymous realities of industrialization. While Gothic Revival became the most popular style of architectural escapism across mainland Europe, the Nordic countries created their own style called National Romanticism. One of its chief exponents was Ragnar Östberg, whose fame rests on the muscular shoulders of his monumental town hall in Stockholm. Constructed from over 8 million dark red *munktegel* (monk's bricks), commonly used for Swedish monastic structures, the hall took 12 years to complete, using traditional techniques and the kind of handiwork championed by the Arts and Crafts movement. The design contains many foreign influences, from medieval Italian palazzos to Venetian waterside residences, and yet manages to be more Swedish than the sum of its parts. Educated at Stockholm's Royal Academy of the Arts, Östberg took inspiration from the city's many lanterns, capping the hall's 106 m (350 ft)-tall tower with his own interpretation, embellished with the national symbol of a gilded Tre Kronor. Ironically for a monument with such nationalistic aspirations, Östberg's town hall proved highly influential overseas, inspiring a generation of brick-built, tall-towered power stations, factories, libraries and civic buildings across Britain, the Netherlands and the United States. **PC**

Ott Carlos

Dates: Born 1946   **Nationality:** Uruguayan   **Location:** Paris, France   **Date Completed:** 1989   **Style | Movement:** Contemporary Modern

In a city such as Paris, modern can mean controversial: this is certainly true of Carlos Ott's new opera house. It was one of the *grands projets* of the then-president of France, François Mitterand, who also personally chose the 1983 winner of the worldwide competition to build a new opera house in Paris in time to commemorate the bicentenary of the French Revolution, on July 14, 1989. Ott, who studied at the University of Hawaii and Washington University School of Architecture in St Louis and who today works out of Canada, produced a massive 30-storey building (ten below ground), with three auditoriums, the largest of which seats 2,700. The rest of the building is dedicated to backstage areas, workshops and all of the infrastructure necessary to support grand-opera productions. The blue granite, glass and steel structure has been likened to a beached whale, but it has had its admirers, too: Ott was awarded the Légion d'honneur in 1988. Since then, he has worked in Germany, Abu Dhabi, South America and China, and is one of the most respected architects practising today. **SF**

Otto Frei

Dates: Born 1925   **Nationality:** German   **Location:** Munich, Germany   **Date Completed:** 1972   **Style|Movement:** High Tech

A student of natural, lightweight structures, Frei Otto is the world's foremost designer of architectural membranes. The unique flexibility of membranes allows them to be used in virtually unlimited ways, with fewer supports and less material than other kinds of structures, and Otto has used them to produce soaring, innovative roofs all over the world. Having studied architecture in Berlin, he served in the Luftwaffe at the end of World War II and ended up in a Russian prisoner-of-war camp. After the war, he set up practice in Germany, and later that decade he taught at Washington University in St Louis. He designed West Germany's pavilion at the Montreal Expo of 1967, and teamed up with Günter Benisch to produce the sweeping tensile structure that flowed over the site of the 1972 Summer Olympics in Munich. Said to imitate the Swiss Alps, the structure is suspended over much of the site—the swimming pools, the gymnasium and the spectacular Olympic Stadium. Plexiglas scales covered a net of tensile steel cables to produce an impressive roof that is still in use today. The stadium had a capacity of 80,000, and also hosted the 1974 World Cup Final and 1988 European Championship Final. **SF**

Dates: Born 1943   **Nationality:** English   **Location:** Isle of Dogs, London, England   **Date Completed:** 1988   **Style | Movement:** Postmodern

After attending Regent Street Polytechnic and the Architectural Association, John Outram started practising architecture in London in 1973. He made his name with the New House in Sussex, England, which won the Best Country House Since The War Award in 1989, given by the *Sunday Times*, who observed, 'When people see a John Outram building, their immediate response is to wave and cheer.' He is particularly noted for his use of colour in projects such as the Egyptian House (also known as Sphinx Hill). In the 1980s the London Docklands Development Authority awarded three storm water pumping station contracts, one of them to Outram, who produced a monumental temple, designed to 'situate one within the cosmos'. (The other two went to Sir Nicholas Grimshaw and Richard Rogers.) Outram's complicated designs reference architecture historically, environmentally and philosophically. In the Pumping Station, the result is a colourful *mélange* of references: glazed blue-green roof tiles, jutting red rafter ends, and sloping walls of banded, red and brown brick. Squat, Egyptian-topped columns and a huge triangular pediment dominate higher levels of dark blue brickwork. More recent works include converting the Addenbrooke's Hospital in Cambridge into the Judge Business School and Duncan Hall for Rice University, Houston, Texas. **SF**

Palladio Andrea (Andrea di Pietro della Gondola) Villa Almerico Capra | La Rotonda

Dates: 1508–80   **Nationality:** Italian (born Padua)   **Location:** Vicenza, Veneto, Italy   **Date Completed:** 1585   **Style | Movement:** Classical

Born in Padua, apprenticed to a stonemason, Andrea Palladio had the good fortune to be taken on to help Gian Giorgio Trissino work on his villa. Trissino fostered his protégé's career and in so doing helped create one of Europe's most influential architects. Palladio's *oeuvre* was limited to north Italy, but—in part due to the Grand Tour and in part due to *The Four Books of Architecture*, his catalogue of work—his reputation spread worldwide. He influenced such luminaries as Sir Christopher Wren

and Thomas Jefferson, whose Monticello owes much to Villa Capra. From majestic churches to glorious palaces—not to mention around 30 villas, including the airy Villa Emo and Villa Foscari, more commonly known as La Malcontenta, as well as the inspirational Villa Capra—Palladio fused classical architecture with landscape in a timeless, simple way that still feels fresh today. La Rotonda, built for cleric Paolo Almerico, sits on a small hill just outside Vicenza with wonderful views of the surrounding

countryside. Both priest and architect died before the building was completed, and it was finished by Vincenzo Scamozzi after Palladio's death—as was Palladio's iconic Teatro Olimpico. The design of Villa Capra changed slightly because of this transition: Palladio's dome was altered and completed with a cupola. **SF**

Dates: Born 1949   **Nationality:** English   **Location:** Majorca, Spain   **Date Completed:** 1991   **Style|Movement:** Minimalism

This minimalist's minimalist has drawn attention well outside of the architectural discipline. John Pawson's limestone-and-glass Calvin Klein flagship store on Madison Avenue in Manhattan attracted the attention of the Cistercian order, who asked him to design a monastery in the Czech Republic. On seeing his plans, they initially worried it was too austere even for them, but they decided to go ahead, and Nový Dvůr was completed in 2004. In the late 1980s Pawson, then in collaboration with the Italian architect Claudio Silvestrin, was commissioned by a German art dealer to design a holiday home on Majorca. Sited high on a hill above almond groves and with a view to die for, the Neuendorf House is textbook minimalism. A straight, stepped, stone path leads up to a forbidding reddish (rendered with local soils) block-like building, reminiscent of a medieval stronghold. Entrance is gained through a slit that leads into an open courtyard, which in turn reveals the geometric villa. Thick walls are pierced with a scattering of small deep windows, which manipulate the light and keep the air cool. Local limestone is used throughout for floors and fittings such as basins, benches and monumental tables. From a glass-walled dining area, a long, narrow pool dissappears towards the horizon. **SF**

Pei Ieoh Ming (I.M.)

Dates: Born 1917   **Nationality:** Chinese / American   **Location:** Paris, France   **Date Completed:** 1989   **Style | Movement:** Modern

Despite being the architect of many public buildings, such as the John F. Kennedy Library, the National Center for Atmospheric Research in Colorado, the Museum of Islamic Art in Doha and the Bank of China's striking skyscraper in Hong Kong, I.M. Pei only became a household name after the unveiling of his pyramids for the Louvre in Paris. Celebrated for his fusion of Asiatic and European architectural traditions in modern buildings, the Chinese-born American architect was not the obvious answer to the problems surrounding the heritage aspects of the Louvre. Pei was asked to provide a modern visitor entrance for the iconic museum and devised a completely unexpected answer with his pyramids. The magnificence of the Second Empire setting is not compromised nor are the views obscured by the structures. Instead, the pyramids subvert the setting and transform the space into both a historic reference and an ultramodern concourse. Situated in the centre of Cour Napoléon, the pyramids are constructed from interlinked steel and covered with light, ochre-tinted, reflective glass. Visitors enter through the main pyramid and descend into a subterranean cavern that contains the reception area and galleries. Further light and ventilation is provided by three similar but smaller pyramids as well as an underground inverted pyramid. **SF**

Peichl Gustav

Kunst-und Ausstellungshalle der Bundesrepublik Deutschland

Dates: Born 1928   **Nationality:** Austrian   **Location:** Bonn, Germany   **Date Completed:** 1992   **Style|Movement:** Postmodern

Originally a designer in the International modern style, Viennese architect Gustav Peichl changed his approach in the 1960s to encompass a more contemporary idiom. This change, first seen in the Rehabilitation Centre for the Mentally Retarded at Vienna-Meidling (1967), veered strongly towards a machine aesthetic with the Austrian State Radio (ORF) regional studios at Salzburg and Eisenstadt, where he used exposed shiny metal-work as a signature element. Peichl describes his hard-to-categorize architecture as being 'the sum of function, material, colour, light, space and volume'. In the late 1980s, Peichl won an international competition to design a new cultural exhibition centre in Bonn, specifically intended to be a forum for a 'dialogue between culture and politics,' with a design tailored to be as flexible as possible with a variety of small, medium and large rooms. The Kunst-und Ausstellungshalle der Bundesrepublik Deutschland is basically a cube fronted by 16 reddish-brown steel columns to represent the 16 states (Bundesländer) of the Federal Republic of Germany. Three light spires on the landscaped rooftop garden symbolize architecture, painting and sculpture, and illuminate the spaces beneath. These include three exhibition halls, a 500-seat auditorium, a foyer and numerous offices, a library, a restaurant and shops. **SF**

Pelli César

Dates: Born 1926 **Nationality:** Argentinian / American **Location:** Kuala Lumpur, Malaysia **Date Completed:** 1994 **Style|Movement:** Modern

One of the biggest boasts in architecture is holding the title for the tallest building in the world. Between 1998 and 2004, this much-coveted appellation belonged to the Petronas Towers, which took a tremendous effort of construction: after over a year of groundworks, the world's deepest foundations were laid in a continuous concrete pour, which took 54 hours for each tower. To save on steel costs, the towers are made from a radical design of high-strength reinforced concrete as well as steel and glass. Despite the height, the elevator takes just 90 seconds to journey from bottom to top. Architect César Pelli incorporated myriad aspects of the local culture into the design. In silhouette, the 88-floor buildings, which have 32,000 windows, resemble the letter 'M' for Malaysia, with a skybridge sitting between them at the 42nd floor. Up close, jagged edges allude to basket weaving, a traditional Malaysian handicraft. Each tower's floor plan resembles a Malaysian Islamic eight-pointed star. The facade is designed to resemble Islamic art motifs, and its subtle green-coloured steel clad-ding refers to the green livery of the Petronas oil company. Pelli's other works include the TWA Terminal at JFK Airport, the United States embassy in Tokyo, and the Canary Wharf Tower in London. **SF**

Perret Auguste

Church of Notre Dame du Raincy

Dates: 1874–1954 **Nationality:** French (born in Belgium) **Location:** Paris, France **Date Completed:** 1923 **Style|Movement:** Modernist

Despite ancient Roman precedents like the Pantheon, concrete was considered an avant-garde material for sacred architecture when Auguste Perret began experimenting with it in the 1890s. The son of a successful stonemason and building contractor, he entered Paris's École des Beaux-Arts in 1891, but left before graduating to join the family firm. Together with his brother Gustave, he began to develop his own vocabulary of reinforced concrete assemblies, which grew ever bolder in their naked expressions of construction. Designed along classical lines, their early apartment building on Rue Franklin, Paris (1904) had a clearly visible grid of rectangular frames, made less confronting to bourgeois tastes with floral patterned infill panels. Perret abandoned such stylistic fig leaves with his triumphant church at Notre Dame du Raincy, whose stripped-backed concrete skeleton was in tune with post-World War I austerity. Its barrel-vaulted aisle is flanked by slender concrete columns, dividing 12 shallow-arched bays. The delicate concrete traceries of the walls melt away amidst the glowing colours of Marguerite Huré's stained-glass inserts, which are suspended in the lattice like translucent cloisonné enamel. Though later eclipsed by his one-time assistant, the brilliant Le Corbusier, Perret remains one of the first architects to let the concrete structures of the buildings see the light of day. **PC**

Piano Renzo

Dates: Born 1937 **Nationality:** Italian **Location:** Nouméa, New Caledonia **Date Completed:** 1998 **Style | Movement:** Eco High Tech

The official jury citation for the 1998 Pritzker Prize was fulsome in its praise of Renzo Piano, comparing him to 'those two earlier masters of his native land, Leonardo da Vinci and Michelangelo'. Held in high regard by his peers, Piano's prodigious output is staggering in its scope, scale and style—ranging from vast airports to intimate art galleries—but his work consistently displays great sensitivity to structure and materials. Together with Richard Rogers, Piano shot to fame in 1971 with the Georges Pompidou Centre, an industrial powerhouse of a museum with an exposed frame and beautifully detailed cast steel components. He founded the Renzo Piano Building Workshop in 1981 and since then has continued to seek a synthesis of art, architecture and engineering, as exemplified by the Jean-Marie Tjibaou Cultural Center. A gift from the French government to help preserve the local, native culture, Piano's design drew inspiration from the mid-point in the construction of the conical thatched huts of the Kanak people of New Caledonia. He created a series of horseshoe clusters, made from laminated iroko hardwood ribs and bound together with polished stainless-steel ties, to form shelters for the study facilities behind. It was a typically Piano composition of tradition, craftsmanship and computer-aided design all melded seamlessly into one. **PC**

Plečnik Jože

Dates: 1872–1957   **Nationality:** Slovenian   **Location:** Prague, Czech Republic   **Date Completed:** 1932   **Style | Movement:** Regional Neoclassicism

Born within the cultural melting pot of the Austro-Hungarian Empire, Jože Plečnik forged a unique style that fused elements of Classical and Byzantine antiquity with the folk traditions of his native Slovenia. He trained in the imperial capital of Vienna under the famed Secessionist architect, Otto Wagner, for whom he worked until 1900. Having experimented with his mentor's avant-garde Art Nouveau style, Plečnik decided to return to the classical orders in search of a sense of continuity and

national identity. This preoccupation became highly pertinent following World War I, as the fragments of empires emerged as fledgling states. Having chosen to settle in Prague, Plečnik accepted a commission from President Tomáš Masaryk in 1920 to design a democratic seat of government for the new Czechoslovakia. Plečnik remodelled Prague Castle as a ceremonial centrepiece, but also created entirely new monuments, such as the Church of the Sacred Heart, which epitomizes his modern twist on

ancient precedents. Based loosely on a classical basilica, its headstone-like bell tower contains ramps on which parishioners can ascend, visible from the exterior through its monumental glazed clock faces. Though neglected for two decades after his death, the advent of postmodernism brought Plečnik a new generation of admirers who recognized his genius for putting old forms to new uses. **PC**

Dates: 1891–1979 **Nationality:** Italian **Location:** Milan, Italy **Date Completed:** 1970 **Style|Movement:** Modernist

A man of seemingly boundless energy and enthusiasm, Gio Ponti was the driving force behind the post-war boom in Italian design. A prolific creator across many disciplines, he studied architecture at the Politecnico in Milan, then became art director for the ceramics firm Richard-Ginori, where he transformed their output by applying neoclassical motifs to simple forms. Having won the firm a Grand Prix at the 1925 Paris Expo, Ponti gradually turned back to architecture, designing houses in Paris and Milan before winning the prestigious commissions for the Mathematics Department of Rome University (1934) and the headquarters of Montecatini (1936). All the while he was editing and contributing to *Domus*, Europe's most influential design magazine, which he had founded in 1928, and which he used to advocate the retention of pattern and decoration within modern design. Ponti's own eclectic output spanned many styles and scales, from the chromed curves of his iconic La Pavoni coffee machine (1948) to the tapered wedge of the Pirelli Tower (1956). Above all, he rejoiced in the application of colour, pattern and texture, as exemplified by his offices for Montedoria, clothed in three-dimensional green ceramic tiles. With their crisp facets enlivening every surface as they catch the changing light, they reflect Ponti's rich take on modernity. **PC**

Prince Bart

Dates: Born 1947   **Nationality:** American   **Location:** Corona del Mar, CA, United States   **Date Completed:** 1989 (additions added later)   **Style | Movement:** Organic

Patronage and pupillage can both play pivotal roles in architects' careers; for Bart Prince the two have been intertwined. Inspired by the late organic works of Frank Lloyd Wright, Prince enrolled at Arizona State University in 1965 to study architecture. A six-month travel award spent helping to plan new town Cwmbran in Wales left Prince convinced that only an organic design approach could help structure new communities. He produced a short book outlining his ideas, which drew the attention of visiting lecturer and leading organic architect, Bruce Goff. Goff had been a friend of Frank Lloyd Wright and the two shared a common client, in the wealthy family of Harold C. Price who owned an oil pipeline business. Prince became Goff's chief assistant in 1970 and, after Goff's death in 1982, he completed a study centre for Japanese art commissioned by Harold Price's youngest son, Joe. Pleased with the result, Joe Price asked Prince to design the house that was to establish his reputation for bespoke residences. Free-form in plan and finish, with deeply contoured layers of cedar shingles and a futuristic timber staircase bristling with stylized branches, the Price House displays a dedication to organic design and detailing that would have pleased both Wright and Goff. **PC**

Pugin Augustus

Dates: 1812–52 **Nationality:** English **Location:** Cheadle, Staffordshire, England **Date Completed:** 1846 **Style|Movement:** Gothic Revival

In the latter years of Queen Victoria's reign, popular taste in architecture and decor became increasingly elaborate. Neo-medieval detailing was the height of good taste and decorated spires, trefoils, gargoyles and stained glass appeared on new buildings the length and breadth of Britain. The greatest exponent of the style was Augustus Pugin. While the gothic ornamentation of the Palace of Westminster is his most visible memorial, Pugin converted to Roman Catholicism in 1834 and much of his work was ecclesiastical. His masterpiece is St Giles's Roman Catholic Church in Cheadle, which was the pet project of the wealthy 16th Earl of Shrewsbury, John Talbot: construction took six years and much of his fortune, and levied a severe physical toll on the workaholic Pugin. Built from local red sandstone, it has a steep roof topped with cast-iron finials and 60 m (200 ft) spire. At the west entrance, a gothic arch holds a red English oak door decorated with two huge gilded hinges formed into rampant lions. Inside, virtually every surface is richly ornamented with pattern and colour, from the encaustic-tiled floor to the elaborate carved-oak roof, with painted walls, colourful stained glass and an elaborate brass rood screen. Most of the work was done—at the earl's insistence—by local tradesmen. Pugin said, 'Cheadle perfect Cheadle, my consolation in all my afflictions.' He literally worked himself to death and died aged 40. **SF**

Rastrelli Bartolomeo Francesco

Dates: 1700–71 **Nationality:** Italian / Russian **Location:** St. Petersburg, Russia **Date Completed:** 1756 **Style|Movement:** Russian Baroque

Bartolomeo Francesco Rastrelli brought Italian sophistication and Baroque extravagance to Imperial Russian architecture by successfully combining fashionable western European aesthetics with local architectural traditions. As senior court architect for Tsarina Anna and then Tsarina Elizabeth, he designed grand palaces and churches, such as Jelgava Palace, Peterhof Palace near St Petersburg, and the Hermitage Pavilion. Rastrelli's grandest work was arguably for the Winter Palace in St Petersburg, a vast structure with approximately 1,060 rooms. Tsarina Anna originally commissioned him to rebuild and enlarge the Apraksin Palace, a project that ultimately became incorporated into the fourth version of Peter the Great's Winter Palace, although Rastrelli only drew up the final plans in 1753 during the reign of Tsarina Elizabeth. Russia was already suffering through the Seven Years War but the empress still levied crippling taxes on her starving people to pay for the project. The rectangular palace contains an inner courtyard and the facade is composed of turquoise walls, white columns and golden sculptures, an entire vista situated underneath a roof studded with urns and figures. The opulent interior holds the Golden Enfilade of stunning state rooms, which runs the length of the palace and includes the 'eighth wonder of the world', the Amber Room, looted in World War II but reconstructed. **SF**

Rietveld Gerrit Thomas

Dates: 1888–1964 **Nationality:** Dutch **Location:** Utrecht, Netherlands **Date Completed:** 1924 **Style | Movement:** De Stijl / Modernist

A frequent criticism of modernist architecture is that its pure forms dictate how people must live within it. The opposite is true of the Rietveld Schröder House for its design was driven by its owner's wish to be close to her three children. The recently widowed Truus Schröder-Schräder commissioned the house from Gerrit Rietveld, a designer and cabinet-maker who had previously refurbished a room in her marital home. A member of the avant-garde De Stijl group, Rietveld had never designed a building before, but he boldly applied the same guiding principles of abstracted planes and primary colours employed in his famous Red and Blue chair (1917). From the outside, the house appears to be in an exploded state of flux, with flat planes that appear to be sliding past each other. The interior builds upon this theme, with an open-plan attic floor whose ingenious sliding and revolving partitions allow for its speedy subdivision into different permutations of rooms. Client and designer worked very closely together and a long-term romance blossomed, leading to Rietveld eventually moving into the house he had helped create. Though his later work would come to focus on functionality and standardization, Rietveld's greatest fame lies with his bespoke house, which proved that modernism could be responsive to the lifestyles of its residents. **PC**

Dates: Born 1933 **Nationality:** English / Italian **Location:** London, England **Date Completed:** 1984 **Style | Movement:** High Tech

It is a common modernist convention for a building to express its inner structure externally, but Richard Rogers made his reputation by taking this a step further and turning his projects entirely inside-out. With his then-partner, Renzo Piano, Rogers attracted world-wide attention in 1971 with a dramatic, competition-winning scheme for the Georges Pompidou Centre in Paris. Their concept was to create an arts centre with complete internal flexibility by banishing all structure and services to its exterior, leaving large, open floor plates. With its massive gantry-like frame, festooned with brightly painted pipework, the design enraged conservative opinion and became an early icon of High Tech architecture. Returning to London without Piano, Rogers's next commission took the externalization of services to new extremes. The new Lloyd's Building shocked the Square Mile with its forest of stainless steel ducts and staircases: these were prefabricated off-site then craned into place on the six service towers that ring the central trading atrium. An economic engine house, the overtly industrial aesthetic of Rogers's early work at Lloyd's has been gradually replaced with more sensuous styling, such as the swooping wooden ceiling of his Barajas Airport (2006), but his office remains committed to highly engineered solutions that clearly express the divisions of a building's core functions. **PC**

Rossi Aldo

Dates: 1931–97   **Nationality:** Italian   **Location:** Maastricht, Netherlands   **Date Completed:** 1995   **Style|Movement:** Architectonic

The multi-talented Aldo Rossi is internationally celebrated for the theories he outlined in his most famous book, *The Architecture of the City*, almost as much as he is for his buildings. One of Rossi's themes is 'repetition and fixation': a search for essential forms that people return to time and again as backdrops for the rituals of life. One early public project to explore these themes was the extension of the cemetery of the city of Modena, which Rossi transformed into, in effect, a city of the dead. A cupola that resembles a science-fiction rocket tops Rossi's Bonnefantenmuseum, and it has punctuated the skyline of Maastricht since the building was completed in 1995. Located on a former industrial estate beside the River Maas, the museum comprises a four-storey, E-shaped building and an independent tower. A hidden skeleton of concrete and steel is clad with traditional materials, in particular brickwork, natural stone and zinc, the latter primarily used in the tower. Rossi conceived the project as an architectural promenade, along which visitors would be guided instinctively through the light-filled galleries. The ground floor is principally public, with galleries on the upper floors. The central staircase is reminiscent of a bright but covered street, and the entire building is suffused with light. **SF**

Rudnev Lev

Dates: 1885–56　**Nationality:** Russian　**Location:** Moscow, Russia　**Date Completed:** 1953　**Style | Movement:** Totalitarian / Stalinist

Lev Rudnev first came to public prominence after the February Revolution, when he won the competition to design the Victims of the Revolution monument in Petrograd. The avant-garde design is a rectangle of terraced granite walls, covered with memorial inscriptions to the 184 citizens buried there. Following the Great Patriotic War (as Russians call World War II), Rudnev was instrumental in rebuilding the badly ravaged cities of Stalingrad,

Riga, Voronezh and Moscow, as well as designing many monumental Soviet buildings. Rudnev was appointed chief architect for the Lomonosov Moscow State University, on a high plateau on Lenin's Hills by the banks of the Moskva river. The imposing building was designed to encourage the joy of life, according to Rudnev, who also insisted that 'the air surrounding the building is no less part of the composition than the construction itself'.

It is Soviet Baroque at its brashest, built by (mostly German) prisoners of war. The central 36-storey tower was the tallest building in Europe until 1990. Said to contain 5,000 rooms, the tower and its four flanking wings are decorated with giant statues, clocks, thermometers, barometers, Soviet crests and wheat sheaves. The huge star on top of the tower contains a small room and viewing platform. **SF**

Rudolph Paul

Dates: 1918–97   **Nationality:** American   **Location:** Hong Kong, China   **Date Completed:** 1987   **Style | Movement:** Postmodern

As a young architect of 35, Paul Rudolph designed the Umbrella House (1953), a combination of passive environmental design and modern flair that won him much acclaim. Rudolph became one of the key figures of what was called the 'Sarasota style'—as exemplified by the Sanderling Beach Club, a light and airy complex perfectly in touch with its suroundings. In 1957 he left Florida to become the dean of the Yale School of Art and Architecture in Connecticut. In 1963, Rudolph completed a new building for the school, one of several divisive, Brutalist public buildings, which were celebrated for their highly complex floor plans and ribbed 'corduroy' concrete, but criticized as being impersonal and inflexible. Finding work hard to come by in the United States but plentiful in the Far East, Rudolph built most of his later buildings there. His first Eastern venture was The Concourse office tower in Singapore, followed by the Bond Centre in Hong Kong, now known as the Lippo Centre. Set on a four-storey podium and apparently propped up on massive concrete legs, two near-identical twin towers are clad from top to bottom in dark blue reflective glass. The project was quickly dubbed the 'Koala Tree', because it looks as if bears are climbing the twin towers, an effect created by regular banks of cantilevered windows, called sky-rooms. **SF**

Saarinen Eero

Dates: 1910–61 **Nationality:** American **Location:** John F. Kennedy (formerly Idlewild) Airport, New York, NY, United States **Date Completed:** 1962 **Style|Movement:** Modernist

Eero Saarinen is famous for his stylistic diversity, but his most iconic works are sensuously sculptural. Son of the famous Finnish émigré architect and educator, Eliel Saarinen, he grew up in the progressive environment of the Cranbrook Academy of Arts in Michigan, where his father was director. Saarinen attended Cranbrook himself, taking sculpture and furniture classes, then travelled to Paris and completed a degree in sculpture before returning home to study architecture at Yale. The young Saarinen formed a close friendship with two of Cranbrook's most gifted students, Charles and Ray Eames. Working together, they created a series of moulded-plywood chairs that scooped the top prizes at the 1940 'Organic Design in Home Furnishings' competition in New York. Keen to do away with the tangle of chair legs, Saarinen went on to design the space age 'Tulip' chair (1956), which balances on a single, slender wineglass stem. The terminal he designed for the Trans World Airlines terminal at Idlewild airport (now the JetBlue terminal at the renamed John F. Kennedy airport) possesses a similar futuristic aesthetic, and the flowing curves of its thin concrete shells meet above a ticket hall where floors, walls and ceilings all blend into one. Completed the year after his death, the terminal remains a fluid memorial to a man who could make concrete take flight. **PC**

Saarinen Eliel

Dates: 1873–1950   **Nationality:** Finnish / American   **Location:** Helsinki, Finland   **Date Completed:** 1919   **Style|Movement:** Early Scandinavian Modern

At the turn of twentieth century, rapid advances in the industrialized world began to suggest new forms and materials for building, accelerating the pace at which architectural styles fell in and out of favour. Eliel Saarinen unexpectedly found himself on the wrong side of modernity in 1904 with his competition-winning design for Helsinki's new railway station. It followed the romantic, rusticated pattern of his winning plan for the National Museum of Finland (1910), which had received great acclaim just two years earlier. But this time Saarinen faced a backlash, led by the architects Sigurd Frosterus and Gustaf Strenell, who called for 'a style of iron and commonsense' in place of idealized re-imaginings of Finland's medieval past. Saarinen took stock and, having toured the new Rationalist German railway stations, he began stripping his design of its picturesque trappings. His final expressive composition employed austere granite walls, trimmed with copper details and two monumental pairs of lantern-clasping stone sentinels. A similarly progressive design won Saarinen second place in the competition for the Chicago Tribune Tower (1922) and, seeking to capitalize on its enthusiastic reception, he chose to emigrate to America in 1923, where he was to become the influential director of the Cranbrook Academy of Art. **PC**

Sacchetti Giovanni Battista

Palacio Real de Madrid | Royal Palace

Dates: 1700–64 **Nationality:** Italian **Location:** Madrid, Spain **Date Completed:** 1764 **Style | Movement:** Spanish Baroque

A pupil of the celebrated Italian architect Filippo Juvarra, Giovanni Battista Sacchetti assisted his master with projects for the Duke of Savoy and then went to Spain to supervise Juvarra's designs for the Palacio Granja in Segovia. Concurrently, Sacchetti extended Juvarra's plans for the Royal Palace in Madrid, taking over completely when Juvarra died in 1736. The previous building, the ninth-century Antiguo Alcázar, the old Moorish castle, had burnt down on Christmas Eve 1734 and a new official royal residence was required by King Philip V. Building started in 1738, following plans loosely based on Versailles but built on a square ground plan. The new palace used local granite and Colmenar stone (limestone) to ensure it would not burn to the ground again: the only wood is in the doors and windows. The features of the main facade include balconies for the principal rooms and numerous columns. On the upper balustrade there are statues of Spanish monarchs, as well as figures of ancient Aztec and Inca rulers, a reference to Spain's American dominions. The palace contains around 2,800 rooms and is surrounded with a magnificent landscaped park as well as a plaza and parade grounds. When finished it was the largest royal palace in Western Europe. **SF**

Safdie Moshe

Dates: Born 1938 **Nationality:** Israeli / Canadian / American **Location:** Montreal, Canada **Date Completed:** 1967 **Style | Movement:** Modern

Moshe Safdie was an enthusiastic participant in the considerable societal and artistic changes of the 1960s. Perhaps his most innovative effort was aimed at finding a solution to the problems of mass housing. To this end, Safdie designed cellular housing schemes: prefabricated units, arranged to make best use of light and green space, which also created a pleasing geometric structure that he believed people would want to live in. First expounded in his university thesis and conceived for mass production, this innovative approach became a one-off project called Habitat 67, which was constructed as one of the pavilions for Expo 67 in Montreal, Canada. The building had 15 different plan types and originally created 158 cubical residences made from 354 identical prefabricated concrete units, made on site and variously arranged so as to give every unit a sense of privacy as well as attractive views. The individual residences varied from between one and eight units with between one and four bedrooms. Each possessed at least one terrace on the roof of the apartment immediately below and was connected to the complex through covered walkways. The unique construction ultimately proved difficult to implement and expensive to construct but also highly influential, and it launched Safdie's successful international career, which includes the brilliant Yad Vashem Holocaust History Museum in Jerusalem. **SF**

Bahá'í House of Worship | Lotus Temple

Dates: Born 1948   **Nationality:** Iranian / Canadian   **Location:** New Delhi, India   **Date Completed:** 1986   **Style | Movement:** Expressionist

In 1976, Fariborz Sahba was asked by the international governing body of the Bahá'í community to design their new house of worship for Kalkaji, New Delhi. For the next ten years he dedicated himself to the build, as architect and project manager, describing his role as that of a translator between the Master Architect and those seeking spiritual refuge and inspiration. The lotus is a sacred flower that symbolizes purity and immortality, and Sahba found inspiration for the design in the symmetrical, circular form of a half-open lotus. The 27 'petals' of the temple are constructed in three layers of freestanding white-marble-clad concrete slabs, set in groups around each of the temple's nine sides. The outer petals form nine entrances, nine secondary petals form the reception and nine inner petals form the main worship area. These last have glass and steel skylights at their apex to throw light into the heart of the building. Internally, the lotus has an exposed pre-cast ribbed roof arcing over the worship area, which can accommodate nearly 2,500 people. Saving money from his budget, Sahba used it to build a series of nine ponds around the temple that give the lotus the appearance of floating on water. **SF**

Scarpa Carlo

Dates: 1906–78 **Nationality:** Italian **Location:** San Vito d'Altivole, Italy **Date Completed:** 1978 **Style|Movement:** Postmodern

Time is a recurring theme within the architecture of Carlo Scarpa, who sought to evolve a language of eternal forms that would transcend the boundaries of style and place. This proved to be a pertinent preoccupation, for many of Scarpa's carefully crafted compositions were dedicated to displaying precious objects from the past. He gained a reputation for his sensitive modern interventions within the historic fabric of his sites, such as the medieval ruins of Verona's Castelvecchio Museum, which he restored between 1959 and 1973. By concentrating on the materials and craftsmanship of his new components he was able to create harmony between past and present without resorting to pastiche. Scarpa was a great admirer of Frank Lloyd Wright and, like him, shared a fascination with traditional Japanese design. These twin influences manifested themselves in his distinctive stepped reliefs, cast in concrete or carved in stone, and the elaborate, often exposed junctions between different elements of his designs. Scarpa's masterpiece was the Brion-Vega Cemetery, where he created an exquisitely detailed trio of chapel, tomb and water pavilion, linked by symbolic sightlines and narrow channels of running water. Their mosaic inlays and cast concrete reliefs now resemble ancient ruins, softened by ivy, time and weather. It is here that Scarpa himself now rests for eternity. **PC**

Scharoun Hans

Dates: 1893–1972   **Nationality:** German   **Location:** Berlin, Germany   **Date Completed:** 1963   **Style|Movement:** Expressionist Modernism

Hans Scharoun was already working as a successful designer and member of the Expressionist circle of German architects before World War II. He remained in Germany throughout the war and afterwards was appointed by the Allies to participate in the rebuilding of Berlin. A lifelong socialist, he had grand plans for the city, but the economic depression halted reconstruction. Instead, Scharoun turned to teaching. His main philosophy was that architecture should provide harmony and balance between a building and its location. This is most apparent in his best-known work, the replacement for the destroyed Philharmonic in Berlin. Here, Scharoun put the music itself firmly at the heart of the project—both physically and conceptually. In the main auditorium the musicians assemble on a central podium around which ranks of offset terraces, positioned for optimum acoustic performance, provide seating for about 2,500 spectators. The ceiling was also constructed with close attention to acoustics; it is shaped like a huge marquee with layered ceiling planes angled to amplify the sound. The smaller Chamber Hall seats around 1,200. From the outside the building's ochre metal cladding mimics the irregular profiles of a forested landscape; its points and angular projections were determined by the internal configuration of the spaces inside. **SF**

Schinkel Karl Friedrich

Altes Museum

Dates: 1781–1841 **Nationality:** German **Location:** Berlin, Germany **Date Completed:** 1828 **Style|Movement:** Neoclassical

Surveyor to the Prussian Building Commission, Karl Friedrich Schinkel was charged with redesigning Berlin after Napoleon's troops were driven out of Prussia. So it fell to Schinkel to re-establish national pride through monumental buildings, often in imposing neo-Greek style. King Friedrich Wilhelm IV particularly wanted a public museum to house the royal collection, and he called on Schinkel to design the Königliches Museum—now known as the Altes Museum—on Museum Island in the

River Spree in central Berlin. Schinkel designed a rectangular building enclosing two inner courtyards, set on either side of a rotunda, which provides the main access to the galleries. Set on a deep plinth to keep it above the water table, the building is entered via a grand staircase, which leads visitors through 18 fluted Ionic sandstone columns. These form a long arcade, flanked at each end by corner pilasters; above the entablature sit 18 sandstone eagles. The rotunda, visible behind them, appears

to be square but in fact conceals a two-storey hemispherical dome, modelled on the Pantheon in Rome, and hidden from the outside so as not to compete with the nearby Berliner Dom. Schinkel painted a long mural cycle along the portico and the upper stairwell, but these were destroyed during the war along with most of the museum. However, the museum was the first of the island's post-war restoration projects. **SF**

Scott George Gilbert

Dates: 1811–78 **Nationality:** English **Location:** St. Pancras Station, London, England **Date Completed:** 1873 **Style|Movement:** Gothic Revival

The son of a clergyman, George Gilbert Scott would rise to become the leading church architect of his day and the master of the Victorian Gothic Revival. A prolific restorer of medieval churches, with a passion for richly decorated screens and ceilings, Scott maintained that gothic detailing was equally applicable to secular structures. Having won the competition for the Foreign and Commonwealth Office in a gothic style, he was wrong-footed by the new prime minister, Lord Palmerston, who ruled that only a classical composition was appropriate. Scott's reluctant Italianate redesign was completed in 1868, but he found more than adequate consolation in his triumphant Midland Grand Hotel at St Pancras Station, with its imposing sweep of red brick and stone capped with a forest of turrets and spires. Honoured in his day with a knighthood and the presidency of the Royal Institute of British Architects, Scott's heavy Victorian detailing clashed with twentieth-century modernist sensibilities and many of his buildings narrowly escaped demolition. The public outcry, led by poet John Betjeman, at the potential loss of the Midland Grand was a rallying point in the preservation movement, the success of which can be judged by the listed status of 607 of Scott's buildings: more than any other British architect. **PC**

Scott Giles Gilbert

Dates: 1880–1960 **Nationality:** English **Location:** London, England **Date Completed:** 1953 **Style|Movement:** Modern

When Sir Giles Gilbert Scott became president of the Royal Institute of British Architects in 1933, his profession was in a period of unprecedented turmoil. Inspired by modernist developments on the continent, young architects had begun challenging the conservative historicism that pervaded much of British architecture and the public debate had grown increasingly acrimonious. Scott sought to heal the rift between modernists and traditionalists by using his presidency to advocate a 'middle line', embracing technology without sacrificing the humanizing aspects of architecture. For Scott, this meant applying historic precedents to modern structures and, in the process, producing some of Britain's greatest architectural icons. He derived his ubiquitous red telephone box (1924) from the domed, mausoleum of Sir John Soane, and disguised the steel frame of Battersea Power Station in a cathedral-like mass of brick, crowned with four classically fluted chimneys. The ecclesiastical grandeur of his power stations at Battersea and Bankside was no coincidence, for Scott was continuously refining the design of an unapologetically gothic building: the great Anglican Cathedral at Liverpool, for which he had won the competition in 1902, aged just 22. The red sandstone cathedral was only completed with the extensive concealed use of modern reinforced concrete, 20 years after his death. **PC**

Seidler Harry

Rose Seidler House

Dates: 1923–2006   **Nationality:** Austrian / Australian   **Location:** Sydney, Australia   **Date Completed:** 1950   **Style | Movement:** Modernist

Far from extinguishing the flame of modernism, the Nazis' closure of the Bauhaus in 1933 simply fanned it across the world. Many of the school's staff and students found homes in Britain and the USA but it fell to the young Viennese Jew, Harry Seidler, to transport their ideas to Australia. Emigrating to Britain in 1938, the outbreak of war saw Seidler interned as an enemy alien then shipped to a camp in Canada. Granted parole to study architecture at the University of Manitoba, he won a scholarship to Harvard where he was taught by former Bauhaus masters Walter Gropius and Marcel Breuer. Together with summer classes from their old colleague, Josef Albers, this gave Seidler the multi-disciplinary skills to mould the first modernist house in Australia. He journeyed to Sydney in 1948 to be reunited with his parents and it was his mother, Rose, who gave him his first commission. A classic piece of directly Bauhaus-inspired design, Rose Seidler's house sits perched upon on its steel and sandstone pillars, with its wide glass windows bringing the green of the bush into her living room. From this bold start, her son would spend the next five decades enlarging the nation's modernist landscape as one of Australia's leading architects. **PC**

Semper Gottfried

Dates: 1803–79　**Nationality:** German　**Location:** Dresden, Germany　**Date Completed:** 1878　**Style | Movement:** Neo-Renaissance / Dresden Baroque

Gottfried Semper designed the Hoftheater in his hometown of Dresden for the Saxon State Opera. Completed in 1841, it was quickly regarded as one of the best opera houses in Europe. Wagner premiered many of his works—such as *Tannhäuser* and *The Flying Dutchman*—there, as did Strauss in later years. After taking part in the May Uprising in 1849, Semper had to flee Germany as a wanted man. He wrote highly regarded architectural books while in exile in London and Zurich. An amnesty was granted

to the revolutionaries in 1862, but Semper never returned to Dresden: when his theatre burnt down in 1869, the public insisted that Semper design the replacement and he drew up the plans, but it was his son Manfred who oversaw the build. The frontage of the Semperoper rises in three great tiers with a two-storey grand portico topped by a rotunda supporting Johannes Schilling's panther quadriga, carrying Dionysus and Ariadne. Above the portal are monuments to figures including Shakespeare,

Molière, Sophocles and Schiller. The building was destroyed yet again during the bombing of Dresden in 1945 but a virtually exact replica was rebuilt, opening in 1985. It was adorned with the original statuary, which had been recovered from the old building. In the new opera house, cementing its links with the past, is a bronze bust of Strauss. **SF**

Shaw Richard Norman

Dates: 1831–1912   **Nationality:** British   **Location:** Cragside, Northumberland, England   **Date Completed:** 1877   **Style|Movement:** Victorian Gothic Revivial / Mock Tudor

Richard Norman Shaw made his reputation with gothic-style domestic residences around the London borough of Hampstead. Pioneering a type of concrete construction, he moved late nineteenth-century design away from the High Victorian aesthetic to the simpler Arts and Crafts style. Hugely influential with his contemporaries in both Britain and America, Shaw went on to design houses, a shopping parade, hotel and church around the garden suburb of Bedford Park, a number of residences on Kensington Gore and, in 1887, New Scotland Yard. But it is an earlier work, Cragside, designed for shipping magnate William Armstrong, that was pro-claimed one of the great won-ders of the age and brought Shaw into the public eye. In addition to its architecture, the house is of interest for its innovative use of technology, its dramatic location and the largest rock garden in Europe. It was the first house to use hydroelectric power for lighting the new incandescent lamps. It used a hydraulic engine to power pumps to provide hot and cold water, central heat-ing and a Turkish bath. It had a telephone system and even a passenger lift. Visited by the Crown Prince of Japan and, in 1884, the Prince and Princess of Wales, the interior was fashion-ably Arts and Crafts, and boasted paintings and stained glass by the greatest names of the time, such as Frederic Watts, Evelyn de Morgan and William Morris. **SF**

Siza Álvaro

Dates: Born 1933   **Nationality:** Portuguese   **Location:** Leça da Palmeira, Matosinhos, Portugal   **Date Completed:** 1966   **Style | Movement:** Modernist

Largely unknown outside of his native Portugal until he was awarded the Pritzker Prize in 1992, Álvaro Siza's carefully considered work is deceptively simple. Pared back almost to the point of minimalism, his structures celebrate their context rather than dominating the surrounding landscape. In Siza's view, 'Architects don't invent anything. They just transform reality,' and amidst the rocks of Leça da Palmeira he blurred that reality, so that pool and sea appear to merge with one another. Siza patiently

walked the site himself, recording the location of each rock formation to determine the layout that would require the least blasting, thereby conserving both terrain and budget. The result was a pair of low-lying pools, the larger of which is bordered by simple concrete walls, which snake through the rocks and protrude within the clear blue water of the pool. Siza proved equally adept at preserving man-made landscapes, poignantly retaining the ruins of homes ruthlessly demolished under Portugal's dictatorship

within the fabric of a new social housing scheme in the São Victor district of Porto (1977). Though he has gone on to create many finely detailed modernist buildings, including prominent libraries, museums and galleries, Siza's early works continue to make waves to this day. **PC**

Dates: 1780–1867 **Nationality:** English **Location:** London, England **Date Completed:** 1847 **Style|Movement:** Greek Revival

Londoner Robert Smirke was a pupil of arch-classicist John Soane for a brief period in 1796 and 1797 until they fell out. He went on to acquire his own love of classicism when he went on his Grand Tour, from 1801 to 1805, during which he was particularly overwhelmed by the dignity and simplicity of the Parthenon. In 1823 Smirke was asked to devise an extension for the King's Library for what would become the British Museum. The result was a Greek Revival design for a quadrangular building with ornamental porticoes on the facades and an 8,000 m² (2 acre) inner central courtyard. The southern entrance wing boasted fluted Ionic columns and a large pediment dedicated to *The Progress of Civilization*. Smirke was a pioneer of the use of concrete and cast iron, and he used the former for the base while the latter made up the frame of the building. The walls were built using London stocks and the public facings were clad with Portland stone. The British Museum turned into a huge project lasting 24 years: the East Wing was completed in 1827 and, by 1841, the North Wing and much of the West Wing. The South Wing frontage was finished in 1847. **SF**

Soane John

Dates: 1753–1837 **Nationality:** English **Location:** London, England **Date Completed:** 1824 **Style|Movement:** Neoclassical

The son of an Essex bricklayer, Sir John Soane rose to the pinnacle of his profession through the scholarly study of classical precedents, which he hoped to propagate. A talented student, Soane was awarded a travelling scholarship by the Royal Academy in 1777, which allowed him to undertake the Grand Tour of Europe alongside much wealthier companions. Soane studiously collected both artefacts and contacts including Richard Bosanquet, whose brother Samuel was to become the Governor of the Bank of England. Having initially struggled to find clients upon returning to England, Soane's contacts gained him the crucial post of architect and surveyor to the Bank of England in 1788, and he spent the subsequent 45 years rebuilding the complex with numerous beautifully domed halls and counting rooms. More commissions followed and Soane used his wealth to amass vast numbers of books, paintings, casts and classical antiquaries, gradually buying and amalgamating three houses in London's Lincoln's Inn Fields as his collection outgrew his home. Arranged across every wall and ceiling, these treasures were used as teaching aids for Soane's own students and in 1833 he negotiated an Act of Parliament that has preserved his house in perpetuity, for the benefit of amateurs and scholars alike, as the Sir John Soane's Museum. **PC**

Spreckelsen Johan Otto von

La Grande Arche de la Défense

Dates: 1929–87   **Nationality:** Danish   **Location:** Paris, France   **Date Completed:** 1989   **Style | Movement:** High Tech Modernist

Every president of France wants to leave his imprint on Paris and, no exception to this rule, then-President Mitterand announced a huge sum to finance several *Grands Projets* to mark the bicentenary of the French Revolution in 1989. The biggest of these became La Grande Arche in La Défense, the financial district in western Paris. Danish architect Johann von Spreckelsen, previously only known for a series of Danish churches, won the international competition with a design applauded by Mitterand for its 'purity and strength'. La Grande Arche is a 35-storey office building in the shape of a hollow cube, made primarily from Carrara marble, glass and granite. Its footprint fills a 100m (330 ft) square: its open walls rise 110m (360 ft) and between them hangs 'the cloud'—a white plastic panelled structure suspended by steel cables, designed to reduce wind resistance. It completes the western end of a long axis from the Arc du Carrousel near the Louvre, along the Champs-Élysées and through the Arc de Triomphe. The project was hugely problematic, not least when the accommodation of existing tunnels under the site necessitated the rotation of the building, six degrees off from the axis it terminates. Political red tape finally drove von Spreckelsen to resign and the project was completed by Paul Andreu. **SF**

Dates: 1861–1925 **Nationality:** Austrian **Location:** Dornach, Germany **Date Completed:** 1928 **Style | Movement:** Expressionist

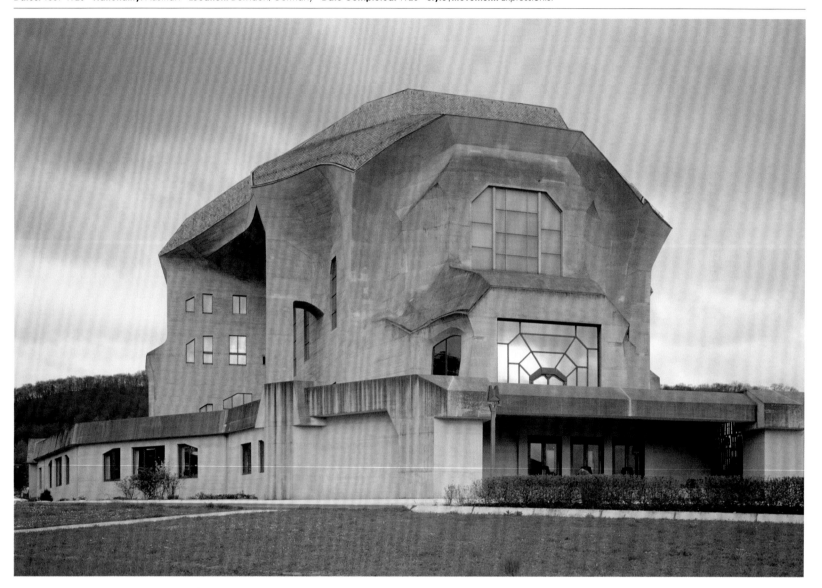

Rudolf Steiner was primarily a philosopher who used architecture as an adjunct to further his idealistic anthroposophical movement. He put his principles into practice with the spiritually expressive forms of his movement's headquarters: the first Goetheanum (after German writer Johann Wolfgang von Goethe) in Dornach. This was a true *Gesamtkunstwerk*, or total work of art, with contributions from a number of artists and craftsmen. Abandoning traditional architectural precepts, Steiner employed boat-builders

to craft the wooden building, but it was destroyed by arson on New Year's Eve, 1922. For the second Goetheanum Steiner worked with modelling clay, finding metamorphic shapes in its plasticity. To replicate these flowing forms he used reinforced cast concrete, pioneering its use, but became too ill to participate much further. It was not finished until three years after his death. Again shipwrights were used, but this time they built the costly shuttering. Completed with magnificent stained-glass windows

lighting the 1,000-seat auditorium and surrounding studios, in it Steiner was again seeking spiritual expression through the use of curved and sculptural forms, which also harmonized with the topography of the nearby Jura mountains. The Goetheanum is celebrated as a masterpiece of Expressionist architecture. Steiner's other architectural works consist of mostly residential buildings in and around Dornach. **SF**

Dates: 1926–92   **Nationality:** Scottish   **Location:** Stuttgart, Germany   **Date Completed:** 1984   **Style|Movement:** Postmodern

Sometimes criticized for not adhering to a consistent style, James Stirling constantly experimented, shifting from the Brutal to the near Baroque. Trained in the Beaux Arts tradition at the University of Liverpool, Stirling formed a practice with James Gowan in 1956, and their Ham Common Flats (1958) were hailed as a landmark in Brutalism for their use of raw concrete and exposed brick. There followed the Engineering Building at the University of Leicester (1963), with distorted masses of red brick and glass, and technological overtones that prefigured the later High Tech movement. Stirling & Gowan dissolved their partnership in 1963 and by the time Stirling partnered with Michael Wilford in 1971 he was already moving towards a monumental style that borrowed heavily from history. Though he rejected the label, Stirling's dramatic hillside Neue Staatsgalerie bore all the hallmarks of postmodernism, with geometric forms of veined sandstone and travertine filled with knowing references, from neoclassical rotundas to the ramped approach to the Acropolis and even the brightly painted pipework of the Centre Pompidou. Dying prematurely following a bungled routine operation, Stirling's legacy lives on through the prestigious Stirling Prize. Its namesake would doubtless be pleased to learn it has been awarded to buildings in a vast variety of styles. **PC**

Sullivan Louis Henry

Bayard-Condict Building

Dates: 1856–1924 **Nationality:** American **Location:** New York City, NY, United States **Date Completed:** 1899 **Style | Movement:** Chicago School

Later adopted as a modernist maxim to justify the eradication of superfluous ornament, the phrase 'Form ever follows function' held a very different meaning for its author. It originally formed part of an 1896 magazine article by Louis Sullivan, entitled 'The Tall Office Building Artistically Considered', in which he called for an appropriate new aesthetic for the first generation of skyscrapers. As a leading member of the Chicago School, Sullivan had great experience in designing tall buildings and his use of advanced steel frame construction freed his walls from their traditional load-bearing role. Sullivan also wished to free them from the trappings of the past, rejecting historical motifs in favour of a new vocabulary drawn from nature, which shared the flowing tendrils of Art Nouveau and the complex interlacing of Celtic strap work. These organic lines suited Sullivan's vertical structures, and he applied them in intense bands across base and cornice, linking the plain slender columns that emphasized the underlying structure. Sullivan's only work in New York City, the Bayard-Condict Building stands in sharp contrast to the mock-historicism of its neoclassical neighbours. The antithesis of modernist minimalism, its 13th floor is wreathed with reliefs of white terracotta foliage, linking angels that soar high above the city streets. **PC**

Tait Thomas Smith

Dates: 1882–1954   **Nationality:** Scottish   **Location:** London, England   **Date Completed:** 1928   **Style | Movement:** Art Deco

Caught between the bright lights of American Art Deco and the earnest purity of European modernism, inter-war British architects often chose to combine elements of both. The versatile Thomas Smith Tait was typical of the period, having no strict allegiance to any one move-ment. He joined the Glasgow firm of John Burnet & Son in 1902, and quickly proved a very talented draughtsman, producing the modern steel-framed design selected by George Eastman for his Kodak Building in London (1911). It owed much to Tait's travels in Detroit and Chicago. A journey to Port Tewfik to study the ruins of ancient Egypt would also bear fruit, in the form of the fantastical facade of the Daily Telegraph Building (1929). With its papyrus col-umns and polychrome clock, it was perfectly in sync with Art Deco fashion, and yet Tait was simultaneously building flat-roofed, cubist-style hous-ing for metal-framed window manufacturers Crittall.

The first modernist housing estate in Britain, Silver End in Chelmsford (1930), showed Tait's future direction, and as a leading partner in the reformed Burnet, Tait & Lorne, he would go on to design many prominent modernist landmarks, culminating in the streamlined St Andrew's House in Edinburgh (1939), which remains the impos-ing seat of the Scottish Government. **PC**

Talman William

Dates: 1650–1719　**Nationality:** English　**Location:** Bakewell, Derbyshire, England　**Date Completed:** 1909　**Style|Movement:** English Baroque

In late seventeenth-century England, William Talman was the most sought-after architect for grand country houses. Although he had a reputation for being difficult, he landed a number of important commissions, including Hanbury Hall in Worcestershire and Uppark in West Sussex. Talman began as a pupil of Sir Christopher Wren but after he became both Comptroller of the King's Works and Superintendent of the Royal Gardens, he wrestled part of the commission to revamp Hampton Court Palace away from Wren, and in 1699 was tasked with completing the state apartments. However, Talman is principally lauded as the architect of Chatsworth House after he was approached by William Cavendish, in 1687, to remodel its south-facing Elizabethan garden frontage. Within two years, Talman gave him a tripartite facade of Baroque magnificence, with luxurious state apartments on the upper levels, all in a style previously only used for royal palaces. Above the rusticated basement, Talman decorated the frontage with a sequence of huge Ionic pilasters, which visually lead to a heavy entablature and classical balustrade decorated with monumental urns. The facade was completed by an elegant double curved staircase, but it was removed in the nineteenth century. The duke then commissioned Talman to remodel the more modest East Front, which he did, between 1689 and 1691. **SF**

Tange Kenzo
Fuji-Sankei Communications Group Headquarters Building

Dates: 1913–2005   **Nationality:** Japanese   **Location:** Tokyo, Japan   **Date Completed:** 1996   **Style | Movement:** Metabolist / High Tech

Japan's post-war embrace of technology and modernity made it a global leader in the fields of electronics and automotive engineering, and the same progressive ethos was reflected in its architecture. The leading Japanese architect of his generation, Kenzo Tange began his career in the offices of Kunio Maekawa, who had previously assisted Le Corbusier. Tange was determined to forge his own identity and though his early works employed Corbusian elements, such as the concrete piloti supporting the floating Hiroshima Peace Centre (1950), they also contained the DNA of traditional Japanese timber-frame construction. Tange's work continued to evolve as he explored highly engineered solutions, leading to the sweeping tensile steel roof of the National Gymnasium for the Tokyo Olympics (1964). Having sculpted these overtly organic forms, Tange then turned to biology at a molecular level and became the figurehead for the Metabolists, an avant-garde group who designed flexible architecture using the model of cells being added or subtracted from living tissue. The two towers of his Fuji-Sankei building are linked by a lattice of aerial walkways, leaving cellular voids free for potential expansion. Caught within this grid, like a giant floating atom, the public observatory makes a statement about Tange's continuous engagement with technology on every scale. **PC**

Terry Quinlan

Dates: Born 1937　**Nationality:** English　**Location:** Richmond, Surrey, England　**Date Completed:** 1987　**Style | Movement:** Classical

Quinlan Terry has the dubious distinction of being very successful but critically regarded as old-fashioned. His preferred style is Classical Palladian and he is much derided by modernists, who label his style 'pastiche'. His clients tend to be institutions, royalty and government: he renovated the interiors of 10 Downing Street for Margaret Thatcher and designed Queen Mother Square in Poundbury, Dorset for Prince Charles's experimental new town. One of Terry's most contentious developments was for Richmond Riverside, a prime site on the River Thames where a series of grand old buildings had been allowed to deteriorate beyond repair. The replacement buildings, which occupy the river frontage and the perimeter of an internal square, appear in a broad mix of classical styles, principally Georgian, but also Greek, Baroque, Venetian gothic and Italianate, and are surrounded by formal public spaces such as the terraces leading to the Thames. The new buildings are also constructed from an equally eclectic range of materials—brick, stone, plaster, concrete: no two buildings are the same—and they thread in and around a number of genuine eighteenth- and nineteenth-century buildings. The complex appears to contain 14 distinct buildings but internally contains many more, including modern open-plan offices, shops and apartments. **SF**

Townsend Charles Harrison

Dates: 1851–1928 **Nationality:** English **Location:** London, England **Date Completed:** 1901 **Style|Movement:** Arts and Crafts

Charles Townsend was a Victorian architect with a distinctly whimsical Arts and Crafts style. His clients were frequently successful businessmen as well as individuals and ecclesiastical institutions looking to make a cultural impact on London. His reputation rests on three great buildings there: the Whitechapel Art Gallery, the Bishopsgate Institute and the Horniman Museum. The latter was funded by tea magnate and MP Frederick Horniman, who assembled an eclectic collection of curiosities during his extensive travels to places including Egypt, Sri Lanka (then Ceylon), Burma, China, Japan, Canada and the United States. Needing a home for his wide-ranging collection, he commissioned Townsend to build him a public museum. The Horniman Museum sits on a slight rise and is built of red brick and Doulting stone from Somerset, much of it carved with tree and foliage reliefs. Townsend spent considerable efforts to ensure that the public could easily flow around the exhibition areas and out into the surrounding grounds. The frontage is dominated by an imposing clock tower that evolves at the top into five richly carved stone circles. The two top-lit barrel-vaulted exhibition halls, which are entered under a huge pastel-coloured mosaic by Robert Bell, feature larger than life-size figures symbolizing humanity and the arts. **SF**

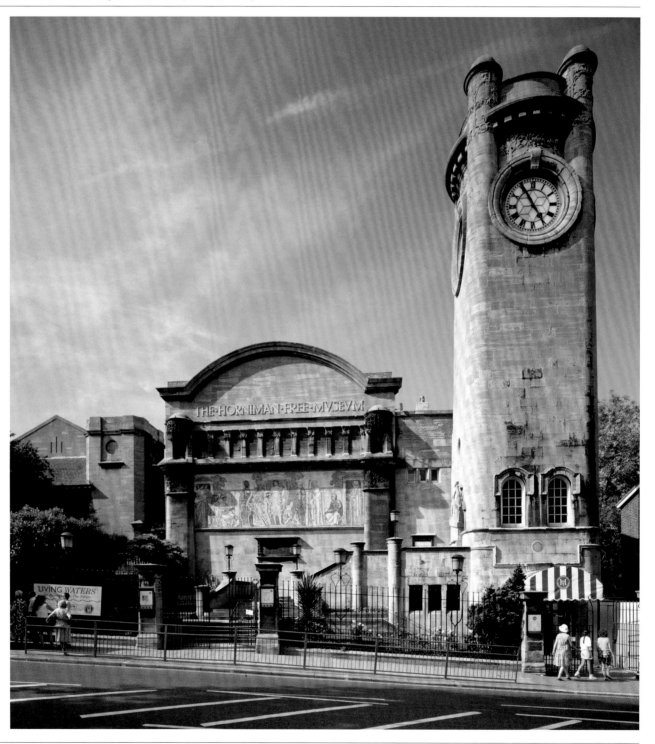

Tschumi Bernard

Parc de la Villette

Dates: Born 1944   **Nationality:** Swiss   **Location:** Paris, France   **Date Completed:** 1989   **Style | Movement:** Deconstructionist

In the late 1970s, Paris embarked on a city-wide regeneration programme. One of the last large parcels of land available for redevelopment was La Vilette, in the northeast, which had been the site of enormous, centralized slaughterhouses. The shambles of old buildings on the 50 hectare (125 acre) site were demolished, and a new urban park was developed by Swiss architect Bernard Tschumi, who won an international competition for the project. Known for theoretical work that insisted on a disconnection between form and use, Tschumi was heavily influenced by Deconstructionist ideas, which were then current in literary and film theory. His design was organized around three superimposed systems: the reference points of 35 unique vermilion steel 'follies', a network of linear paths, and the flat planes of sports fields. Built over a period of 15 years, the Parc de la Villette also included over 25 new buildings, all linked by covered walkways, promenades and bridges. Described by Tschumi as a discontinuous but single building, the park includes playgrounds, workshops, a gymnasium, ten themed gardens and exhibition and concert spaces, as well as the Museum of Science and Technology and the City of Music. On warm summer nights the playing fields become an open-air cinema capable of holding 3,000 people. **SF**

Ungers Oswald Mathias

Dates: 1926–2007   **Nationality:** German   **Location:** Kunsthalle, Hamburg, Germany   **Date Completed:** 1997   **Style | Movement:** Rationalist

Oswald Mathias Ungers is primarily recognized for his inspired urban thinking, although he is also known for his rather severe architecture. Working in the 1960s and 1970s in East Berlin, Ungers argued for prioritizing the acute need for mass housing over the more individual desire for personal space. His designs primarily use simple geometric forms, like cubes and cylinders, which he rearranges to create, in his words, 'clear spaces that touch on the essence of architecture'. Devoted to abstraction,

Ungers had an unusual and uncompromising approach to the context of his buildings, which did not always make him a popular man: his 1964 Märkisches Viertel vertical housing scheme in Berlin received very hostile criticism. Later designs, like the Messe-Torhaus for the trade fair complex in Frankfurt, were better received. In the 1990s Ungers was commissioned to design the Galerie der Gegenwart (Gallery of Contemporary Art) extension for the Kunsthalle in Hamburg, Germany.

To accompany the two older museum buildings, Ungers designed a two-part building: the first level consists of a pedestal of light red granite, above which sits the second structure, a striking, four-storey white limestone-clad cube. Inside it offers 5,600 m² (60,000 sq ft) of exhibition space within a deliberately flexible area. In 2000, he won a competition to renovate Berlin's Pergamon Museum, continuing his success with museums. He died shortly before work started. **SF**

Unwin Raymond

Dates: 1863–1940   **Nationality:** English   **Location:** Hampstead Garden Suburb, London, England   **Date Completed:** 1935   **Style | Movement:** Arts and Crafts

Raymond Unwin was a committed socialist who worked as an engineer before turning his hand to architecture, intending to improve the living standards of the working class. In partnership with his brother-in-law, Barry Parker, he designed residential houses and stripped-down Arts-and-Crafts-style housing estates. Their first big ventures were New Earswick near York for the Joseph Rowntree Village Trust, followed by Letchworth for the Garden City Company. In 1905, social reformer Henrietta Barnett, who shared Unwin's socialist ideals, outlined a plan for a new garden suburb in Hampstead, north London. Unwin was appointed Architect and Surveyor with a brief to provide attractive, mixed-income housing at low-density levels, incorporating allotments as well as existing hedgerows, old trees and woods. Unwin and Parker responded with a homogenous design for groups of attractive houses on gently curving streets, which embraced the existing contours of the ground. The rural atmosphere was reinforced by the use of natural features—such as hedges to define the boundaries between houses. The houses were designed by the best contemporary architects. Sir Edwin Lutyens was consulting architect. He laid out the Central Square and designed many important buildings. After overcoming many restrictions through an Act of Parliament, the result was and continues to be hugely popular, today home to some 13,000 people. **SF**

Ustad Lal Chand

Dates: Unknown **Nationality:** Indian **Location:** Jaipur, India **Date Completed:** 1799 **Style|Movement:** Rajput / Mughal

Little is known about Lal Chand Ustad except that he designed the layout of the Pink City of Jaipur in Rajastan and, within it, the stunning, beehive-like Hawa Mahal (Palace of Winds), in the late eighteenth century. Part of the city palace, Hawa Mahal was completed in 1799 and is actually little more than an elaborate five-storey facade 15 m (50 ft) high, accessible from the harem building behind it. The design is based on the shape of the Hindu god Lord Krishna's crown (*Mukuta*). It was built as a private grandstand for the purdah-restricted wives of the Maharaja Sawai Pratap Singh: carved into red and pink sandstone, less than a foot thick, 953 small latticework *jharokhas* (windows) allowed the women to look out on the street below without being seen. Small patios with a central fountain sit behind the first and second floors, which were reserved for the senior wives, while the top three floors are only one room deep. Hawa Mahal was also used as a royal retreat in the extreme heat, as the latticework screens provoke small, cooling breezes. The back of the facade is a series of colonnades, corridors, balconies and slopes leading to the upper storeys, not as elaborately decorated as the front. **SF**

Utzon Jørn

Dates: 1918–2008   **Nationality:** Danish   **Location:** Sydney, Australia   **Date Completed:** 1973   **Style | Movement:** Expressionist

'A design can grow like a tree. If it grows naturally, the architecture will look after itself.' So Jørn Utzon describes his 'additive architecture'. In 1957, the virtually unknown 38-year old Utzon, championed by Eero Saarinen, won the international competition to create a new opera house for Sydney, Australia, with a unique schematic design. The now-iconic structure with its multiple sail-shaped roofs proved hugely problematic to construct; its exact form was only resolved after construction started. When put

together, the 14 shells of the building would form a perfect sphere—a solution Utzon discovered when peeling an orange. Engineering problems and a too-tight budget as well as poisonous press and hostile politicians forced Utzon to resign from the project in February 1966. The exterior of the building was almost complete but Utzon's spectacular interior was radically altered by local architects before the building was finally completed—massively over budget—in 1973. Sitting on a wide horizontal

platform, the building contains five performance halls under concrete shells clad with white tiles. For decades, Utzon's contribution to the design was downplayed, but in 2000 he was asked to update the interior: his work, christened the Utzon Room, was completed in 2004, the year after he won the Pritzker Prize for his inspired designs. **SF**

Van Alen William

Dates: 1883–1954 **Nationality:** American **Location:** New York City, NY, United States **Date Completed:** 1930 **Style|Movement:** Art Deco

In the late 1920s, New Yorkers were entranced by the rivalry between developers and their architects, vying to build the tallest building in the world. William Van Alen, working for Walter Chrysler, raced a rival team erecting a skyscraper at 40 Wall Street for the Bank of Manhattan. Designed by Van Alen's former partner, H. Craig Severance, that 282 m (925 ft), 71-storey tower was the tallest building in the world when finished in April 1930. It seemed that Severance had won, but Van Alen had secretly assembled a seven-storey stainless steel spire—based on a Chrysler radiator—which, when hoisted into place, gave the Chrysler a winning 318 m (1,045 ft) height. The stunning surprise was hoisted through the roof space and anchored into place in just one and a half hours. Other ornamentation, most notably the eagle gargoyles and steel hubcaps on the building, resembled Chrysler car ornaments. A triumph of Art Deco style both inside and out, the building has a stunning lobby that mixes marble, onyx and amber. For one brief year, the 77-storey Chrysler Building was the tallest building in the world, until it was surpassed by the 102-storey Empire State Building in 1931. The Chrysler remains the tallest brick building in the world. Van Alen did not have a contract with Chrysler and a dispute over payment terms led the architect to sue, successfully, for his fee. This damaged his reputation and ended his career. **SF**

Vanbrugh John

Dates: 1664–1726   **Nationality:** English   **Location:** Woodstock, Oxfordshire, England   **Date Completed:** c. 1722   **Style | Movement:** English Baroque

More a public war memorial than a private mansion, the theatrical martial might of Blenheim Palace unites many strands of Sir John Vanbrugh's eventful life. Commissioned into the army in 1686, Vanbrugh was caught spying in Calais and imprisoned in the infamous Bastille. Upon returning to England he promptly became a popular playwright with such scandalous comedies as *The Provoked Wife* of 1697 before turning to architecture, almost on a whim, when his friend the Earl of Carlisle invited him to design his mansion at Castle Howard in 1699. Vanbrugh's membership of the elite Kit-Kat club gave him a pool of wealthy Whig clients, who helped him obtain the position of Comptroller of Public Works in 1702 despite his having no formal architectural training. His greatest commission was Blenheim Palace, which was to be the grateful nation's gift to the Duke of Marlborough for his famous victory over the French in 1704. Vanbrugh's dramatic inclinations were ideally suited to the flamboyant Baroque, and Blenheim is filled with overt symbolism: British lions maul French cockerels and piles of cannon balls pose as decorative finials. Massive cost overruns forced Vanbrugh to leave the stage in 1717, but Blenheim was faithfully completed by his talented assistant, Nicholas Hawksmoor. **PC**

Velde Henry van de

Van de Velde Building

Dates: 1863–1957   **Nationality:** Belgian   **Location:** Weimar, Germany   **Date Completed:** 1911   **Style | Movement:** Jugendstil

Although he spent much of his career in Germany, the painter, interior decorator and architect Henry van de Velde was one of the leading exponents of Jugendstil in Belgium. He was one of the first architects to consider a building in its entirety, right down to the detailing of lighting and door furniture, coordinating exterior form with interior decoration so that the whole would harmonize seamlessly together. In 1904, van de Velde designed the Grand Ducal Saxon School of Arts and Crafts in Weimar (now the Van de Velde Building),using Charles Rennie Mackintosh's Glasgow School of Art as his inspiration—especially its large light-flooding windows. Designed in the Jugendstil style and constructed mainly from concrete, glass and steel, the building is most remarkable for its central staircase and unconventional lighting. The following year van de Velde designed the School of Applied Arts, which was also built in the Jugendstil tradition. In 1907 the Grand Duke of Saxony asked him to become head of the school. He expounded his utopian ideals to his students, believing that architects could reform society through design and arguing: 'Ugliness corrupts not only the eyes, but also the heart and mind.' He taught architecture and design at the school until 1915, when the war forcd him to return to Belgium. He recommended Walter Gropius to replace him: the latter renamed it the Bauhaus. **SF**

Venturi Robert

Dates: Born 1925   **Nationality:** American   **Location:** Philadelphia, PA, United States   **Date Completed:** 1964   **Style|Movement:** Postmodern

Private houses for family members have provided the launch pad for many architectural careers, but the home Robert Venturi designed for his mother would prove a seminal moment for his whole profession. Born in the same year that Le Corbusier revealed his then-revolutionary Pavilion de L'Esprit Nouveau, Venturi graduated from his architectural studies at Princeton in 1950 to find a world dominated by the uniformity of functional modernism. Frustrated by the banal repetition of

what he saw, Venturi resolved to create architecture much richer in meaning by re-evaluating historical styles and then layering their symbolism into new compositions. He poured his ideas into the Vanna Venturi House, which evolved as a witty montage of domestic vernacular traditions with its gabled roof and central chimney piece revealed by a deep split pediment. The house formed a case study in his book *Complexity and Contradiction in Architecture* (1966), which became the bible of the nascent

postmodernism movement, provoking a counter-revolution that continues to animate and divide the architectural world to this day. Though Venturi's scholarly work provides an academic justification for rethinking applied decoration, it is his pithy parody of Mies van der Rohe's famous austere maxim that summarizes the postmodern perspective most concisely. For Venturi at least, 'Less is a bore'. **PC**

Villanueva Juan de

Dates: 1739–1811   **Nationality:** Spanish   **Location:** Madrid, Spain   **Date Completed:** 1819   **Style | Movement:** Neoclassical

Juan de Villanueva would not recognize his creation today—not because this epitome of Spanish neoclassicism has changed form, but because its function has altered dramatically. Designed in 1785 on the orders of Charles III to house a natural history collection, building was halted during the War of Independence. It was only completed during the reign of Charles's grandson, Ferdinand VII, when it was given a new role as what would become the National Museum of Paintings and Sculptures—from 1868 the Prado Museum (*prado*, meaning meadow, was the name of that area of Madrid). The catalogue for the opening exhibition in 1819 boasted 311 paintings, taken from a collection of over 1,500 pictures. Today, as one of the world's greatest repositories of art—with some three million visitors in 2011—the collection has expanded a hundred times. Although the Prado has also expanded, it mainly did so by incorporating outlying buildings until 2007, when Spanish architect Rafael Moneo's extension altered Villanueva's building significantly, although much of the addition was underground. Most of Villanueva's other work can be seen in Madrid— much of it for the monarchy after 1777, when he was appointed the official architect of the Prince and Princess—where he stamped his neoclassical style on the Royal Academy of History, Oratory of Caballero de Gracia, Royal Botanical Gardens and Plaza Mayor. **SF**

Viñoly Rafael

Dates: Born 1944   **Nationality:** Uruguayan   **Location:** Tokyo, Japan   **Date Completed:** 1996   **Style | Movement:** High Tech Modernist

Few architects have been trusted with such a wide range of prestige projects around the world as Rafael Viñoly. After creating one of South America's largest practices in the 1960s and 1970s, he settled in New York City in 1979, starting Rafael Viñoly Architects in 1983. He says, 'Architecture is a dialogue with the forces of life … its essential responsibility is to elevate the public realm.' In 1989 Viñoly won the international competition to design one of the most important cultural complexes in Japan—the Tokyo International Forum. The Forum resembles an elongated boat made out of soaring arcs of glass and steel. At its heart lies a large granite-paved plaza, which acts as a public space and an entrance point. At the west end a hull-shaped glass and steel atrium rises 60 m (195 ft) high; to the east a cluster of buildings contains theatres, shops and restaurants. The huge atrium is linked to the rest of the complex via walkways enclosed with laminated glass; other metal walkways double as horizontal struts to resist wind pressure on the Glass Hall. The vast, laminated-glass walls and ceiling of the Hall pitch natural light into the subterranean lobby area. Here, two underground levels lead to nearby transport hubs but also contain a range of shops and facilities. The concourse surrounds the central exhibition hall and flows on to become the main floor of the Glass Hall. **SF**

Dates: 1857–1941   **Nationality:** English   **Location:** London, England   **Date Completed:** 1896   **Style | Movement:** Arts and Crafts

Yorkshireman Charles Voysey came from a family of individualists: his father, the Reverend Charles Voysey, lost his living after being prosecuted for heresy. Educated mainly by his father, Voysey the younger also studied under J.P. Seddon and George Davey before setting up his own practice in 1881 at Broadway Chambers in Westminster, London, where he worked at small alterations and surveys. He sold his first pattern design to Jeffery & Co. in 1883. A decorative artist of some note, he joined the Art Workers' Guild in 1884 (becoming a master in 1924) and exhibited at the first Arts and Crafts Exhibition Society show in 1888. Voysey designed some 50 properties, mainly residential, before World War I, but in later years he had few commissions, working increasingly on furniture and decorative fabrics until lack of money forced him to depend on his son. His architecture, influenced by William Morris and Augustus Pugin, is characterized by roughcast walls with stone dressing, buttresses and big tiled roofs—all seen at Annesley Lodge, built for his father. Nikolaus Pevsner dubbed it 'astonishingly ahead of its date' and lauded his work, particularly Voysey's own house, The Orchard, in Chorleywood. Pevsner saw him as an important step on the way to modernism. Voysey disliked this view, but it contributed to his recognition in the 1930s, culminating in his award of the Royal Institute of British Architects' Gold Medal in 1940. **SF**

Wagner Otto

Dates: 1841–1918 **Nationality:** Austrian **Location:** Vienna, Austria **Date Completed:** 1899 **Style | Movement:** Jugendstil

Otto Wagner was born in Vienna and, after studying at the Königliche Bauakadamie in Berlin, returned home to finish his studies at the Academy of Fine Arts. He joined the practice of Ludwig von Förster and, in 1864, started his own practice in Vienna, building private houses in the historicist style, such as the Villa Epstein in Baden. In 1883, he won a competition for a new plan of Vienna, becoming an adviser to the Viennese Transport Commission and the Commission for the Regulation of the Danube Canal. The result was the Stadtbahn, and his work on it lived up to his dictum: 'Nothing that is not practical can be beautiful.' Today, after renovation, the stations have been returned to their former glory and the one at Karlsplatz, a perfect example of the Jugendstil style, houses an exhibition of his work. Wagner was a powerful influence on Viennese architecture as Professor of Fine Arts at the Academy (from 1894), as a writer (publishing *Moderne Architektur* in 1896), and as a member of the Secession movement (from 1897)—many other Secessionists had been his students. He designed several other important works in Vienna, including the Majolica House, the Post Office Savings Bank, the Steinhof Church and the Neustiftgasse apartment block. All are elegantly austere but with significant decorative touches, often by fellow Secessionists such as Koloman Moser, Othmar Schimkowitz and Richard Luksch. **SF**

Walter Thomas Ustick

Capitol Building | wings and cast-iron dome

Dates: 1804–87 **Nationality:** American **Location:** Washington, DC, United States **Date Completed:** 1863 **Style|Movement:** Neoclassical

Founder of the American Institute of Architects and its second president, from 1876 to 1887, Walter made his name in his hometown of Philadelphia, PA, where he worked for William Strickland before setting up his own practice in 1831. In 1833 he designed Girard College's Founder's Hall in Greek Revival style, and later used the Gothic Revival style for two Episcopal churches in North Carolina: St James in Wilmington and Chapel of the Cross in Chapel Hill. In 1851, his plans for the enlargement of the United States Capitol gained approval and President Millard Fillmore appointed him the fourth Architect of the Capitol. He held the position until 1866, overseeing the enlargement of the building by the addition of two marble wings and the replacement of Bullfinch's copper dome with the grand cast-iron version that is visible today. In spite of the outbreak of the Civil War, which forced a cessation of work for around a year, construction continued apace and, in December 1863, Thomas Crawford's statue 'Freedom Triumphant in War and Peace' (today renamed the Statue of Freedom) was lifted to its crowning position. The resulting edifice is one of the most recognizable buildings in the world. **SF**

Dates: 1830–1905 **Nationality:** English **Location:** London, England **Date Completed:** 1881 **Style|Movement:** Gothic Revival

One of the most successful British architects of the Victorian period, Alfred Waterhouse has a legacy that is particularly evident in Manchester and at Oxford, Cambridge and London Universities, and which is also visible in numerous private houses and institutions around the country. He worked in a confidently varying selection of Neo-Gothic, Romanesque Revival and Renaissance Revival styles. Two of his most important buildings are Manchester Town Hall and the magnificent Natural History Museum in South Kensington, London. Waterhouse started working on the latter in 1864 using the German Romanesque style and it was completed by 1883, without the wings he proposed, due to cost. The entire facade is covered with terracotta tiles: cheap, mass-produced, highly durable, washable against the notorious London smog and, crucially, a structural material. Round arches are a repeated motif for all the windows as well as the main entrance, which was inspired by the great columns of basalt in western Scotland. The terracotta entrance hall is reminiscent of a cathedral in its ambition. The entire building, inside and out, crawls and writhes with reliefs of plants and animals: up columns, around the staircase, in niches and crannies. The west zoological wing features living species and the east geological wing those that are extinct. **SF**

Dates: 1849–1930   **Nationality:** English   **Location:** London, England   **Date Completed:** 1909   **Style | Movement:** Victorian

Sir Aston Webb was one of the greatest of the late Victorian architects. He started his own practice in 1874; by the turn of the century it was Britain's largest. Webb's many accolades included the presidency of the Royal Institute of British Architects, from 1902 to 1904, a knighthood in 1904, the AIA's Gold Medal in 1907, the first year it was awarded, and acting presidency of the Royal Academy, from 1919 to 1924. Many of his buildings were designed in partnership with Ingress Bell (1836–1914); they worked together for 23 years from 1886, when they designed the Victorian Law Courts in Birmingham. Webb's works include Admiralty Arch at the east end of the Mall and the Queen Victoria Memorial at the west; the east front of Buckingham Palace; the Royal Naval College, Dartmouth, Devon; the University of Birmingham; and the main building of what became the Victoria and Albert Museum—the name changed in May 1899 when the queen laid the foundation stone in her last public ceremony. Webb had won an 1891 competition with a red brick and Portland stone design incorporating statues of great British artists, architects and craftsmen. It was well-received by the architectural press of the time and has gone on to become a London monument. **SF**

Webb Philip

Dates: 1831–1915   **Nationality:** English   **Location:** Bexleyheath, England   **Date Completed:** 1860   **Style | Movement:** Arts and Crafts

Philip Webb was one of the most important figures in the Arts and Crafts movement. He was a close friend of William Morris, with whom he started the decorative arts company Morris, Marshall, Faulkner & Co. and, in 1877, the Society for the Protection of Ancient Buildings. Webb met Morris in 1856 while they were both employed by Gothic Revivalist architect George Street. Webb taught Morris architectural drawing, and they became friends. Morris, who married Jane Burden in 1859, chose Webb to design a family house for them. Red House was Webb's first job as an independent architect— he had set up his own practice in 1858—and would be hugely influential as one of the earliest examples of Arts and Crafts architecture. He would go on to produce many other country houses in his career. Morris wanted a 'palace of art', and Red House boasted ceiling paintings and wall-hangings by Morris as well as furniture painted by him and Pre-Raphaelite founder Dante Gabriel Rossetti (who would have a long affair with Jane Morris), and stained glass by Edward Burne-Jones. The east front of the red-brick house describes an L-shape around Well Courtyard—the cone-shaped tiled roof of the well is in the centre of the photo— showing off the garden porch and window styles. Sadly, Morris was unable to enjoy the fruits of his labours for long: he had to sell Red House in 1865 after illness. **SF**

Wilford Michael

The Lowry Centre for the Performing Arts

Dates: Born 1938 **Nationality:** English **Location:** Manchester, England **Date Completed:** 2000 **Style|Movement:** Postmodern

Touched by tragedy, but also by success, the performing arts centre at Salford Quays saw Michael Wilford assume the central role within a practice he had been a part of since 1960. Conceived as the centrepiece for the regeneration of the former docks, the Lowry was originally commissioned from the leading British practice of James Stirling and Michael Wilford, who had been in full partnership since 1971. When Stirling died during a routine operation in 1992, it fell to Wilford to complete the design and deliver both the Lowry as well as several other important projects in progress. Wilford shared Stirling's postmodern design approach, marrying simple geometric solids with varied historic and contextual references, and enriching the whole with strong colour and materials. Making clear references to naval architecture, the Lowry's distinctive stainless steel volumes each houses a separate function, incuding the 1,730-seat Lyric Theatre, the smaller 466-seat Quay Theatre and an art gallery that holds the world's largest collection of L.S. Lowry's work, some 430 pieces in all. A popular success, the Lowry received The Royal Fine Art Commission Building of the Year Award in 2001, and the highly experienced Wilford now heads practices in Britain and Germany as well as lecturing at numerous prestigious universities. **PC**

Wilkinson Chris and Eyre Jim

Dates: 1849–1930 **Nationality:** English **Location:** Newcastle-upon-Tyne, England **Date Completed:** 2001 **Style|Movement:** Modern

The Gateshead Millennium Bridge spans the River Tyne between Gateshead and Newcastle, with a simple and graceful functionality. Lifted into place in November 2000 by the huge *Asian Hercules II* floating crane, it was dedicated by Queen Elizabeth II in 2002. The bridge comprises two curves, the deck and its support, which tilt to allow traffic beneath—the curve of the deck necessary to accommodate the traffic increases the crossing distance by 15 m (50 ft). Each 'blink' of this eye takes four minutes,

as 850 tonnes of bridge are tilted by eight electric motors. This unique approach to a pedestrian bridge won architects Wilkinson Eyre the 2002 Royal Institute of British Architects' Stirling Prize, their second in consecutive years, as they had won the 2001 award for their work on the Magna Science Adventure Centre, which was built on a disused steelworks in Yorkshire. Chris Wilkinson went into practice in 1983 and was joined by Jim Eyre in 1986. The partnership, formed in 1987, has been responsible for numerous

eye-catching and innovative designs: their recent Guangzhou International Finance Centre in China—the tallest tower built by a British architect—won the Royal Institute of British Architects' 2012 Lubetkin Prize for the best new international building outside the European Union. **SF**

Dates: 1922–2007   **Nationality:** English   **Location:** London, England   **Date Completed:** 1997   **Style|Movement:** Modernist

Even in the modern age of rapid construction techniques, some projects refuse to be hurried. The career of Sir Colin St John Wilson was dominated by the mammoth 35-year struggle to build a new British Library, which would eventually house upwards of 14 million books. Wilson graduated from the Bartlett School of Architecture in 1949 and went to work for London County Council Architects under the direction of leading British modernist Sir Leslie Martin. He later joined Martin as a member of the

teaching staff at Cambridge University, where he met the Finnish architect Alvar Aalto, whose brand of red brick modernism directly influenced the design of the British Library. Wilson began his Herculean task in 1962, but progress was slowed by changes in site and government, and his 1978 design had to be further revised as budgets were slashed. Wilson's attempts to replicate the humane character of Aalto's architecture were partly thwarted by the sheer scale of the building's

exterior, but his insistence on high-quality materials and natural lighting made the interiors an inspiring place to study. The pleasing patina developing on the library's leather-bound banisters indicates that this dignified public building will gracefully endure in direct proportion to the time Wilson invested in its design. **PC**

Wood the Younger John

Dates: 1728–82   **Nationality:** English   **Location:** Bath, England   **Date Completed:** 1775   **Style | Movement:** Palladian

Bath in southwestern England is both a World Heritage City and a top tourist location. Two prime reasons for this are the Royal Crescent, which was designed by John Wood, the Younger, and the nearby Circus, designed by his father, John Wood, the Elder. One of seven children, John Wood worked closely with his father as his chief assistant, and completed the Circus in 1764 after his father's death. He went on to design the Assembly Rooms (1771), but his best-known work is the quintessential example of Georgian architecture, the Royal Crescent. Built from local oolitic limestone—better known as Bath stone—which weathers to a striking honey yellow, the Crescent (as it was originally termed) boasts 114 Ionic columns and 30 houses. An expansive lawn and Royal Victoria Park ensure unobstructed views down towards the River Avon for the many tourists visiting the Crescent, who can see what life was like in the Georgian period by visiting the museum at No. 1 (on the right of the photograph)—but it is for the perfect Palladian symmetry that most visitors remember the Royal Crescent. Lucky to survive the Baedecker Blitz of April 1942 when bombs gutted two of the houses, the Crescent's uniform facade is only skin deep. Each of the houses behind was designed in conjunction with the prospective owner, accounting for the asymmetric and unruly rear view. **SF**

Wren Christopher

Dates: 1632–1723   **Nationality:** English   **Location:** London, England   **Date Completed:** 1711   **Style | Movement:** Baroque

Mathematician, scientist, astronomer, architect—Sir Christopher Wren was a polymath and one of the greatest men of his age. Undoubtedly well-connected (his father became Dean of Windsor in 1635 and the young Christopher used to play with the Prince of Wales, later his patron, Charles II), Wren went to Oxford University in 1649. He became Professor of Astronomy at Gresham College, London, and joined the scientific discussion group that would become, in 1662, the Royal Society of

London for the Promotion of Natural Knowledge. His architectural career started at this time, with a chapel at Pembroke College in 1663 and the Sheldonian Theatre in Oxford (1664–68). In 1669 he became Royal Architect, and while his plan for the reconstruction of London was not taken up, he designed and built many churches and other important buildings after the Great Fire of London in 1666, assisted by Nicholas Hawksmoor. One of these was St Paul's Cathedral, in many ways the icon of the

capital, even now that its dome, which stood out of the smoke of the Blitz, is surrounded by modern skyscrapers. Started in 1675, after nine years of planning and argument, the fourth cathedral on the site, with its Corinthian columns and spectacular dome, is Wren's masterpiece. Well may his gravestone in the cathedral bear the inscription (in Latin): 'Reader, if you seek his monument look around you.' **SF**

Wright Frank Lloyd

Solomon R. Guggenheim Museum

Dates: 1867–1959   **Nationality:** American   **Location:** New York, NY, United States   **Date Completed:** 1959   **Style | Movement:** Organic

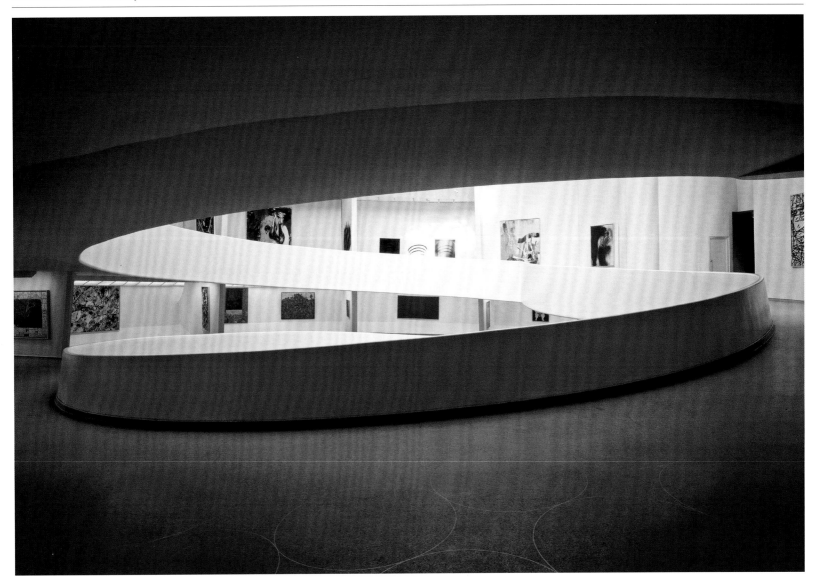

Unquestionably the greatest American architect of the twentieth century, Frank Lloyd Wright's vast output included over 500 realized projects and left a legacy that touches nearly every aspect of his profession. One prevailing theme in Wright's pursuit of an 'Organic Architecture' was his understanding of materials and his ability to exploit them to achieve his goals. Though his early designs were within the brick and timber traditions of the Arts and Crafts movement, he later developed an interest in concrete, exploring its decorative possibilities through his modular Textile Block System, which he applied to the Mayan-inspired Storer House (1923). He later demonstrated the structural properties of concrete, relying on his studies of *staghorn cholla* cacti to design the forest of dendriform columns at the Johnson Wax Headquarters (1939). To the amazement of building inspectors, these thin-walled pillars of concrete and steel mesh proved capable of supporting five times the double safety load their codes required. Wright's vision of a truly organic architecture was triumphantly realized in his final work, the Guggenheim Museum in New York, whose seemingly unsupported spiralling gallery ramp remains one of the world's most sculptural applications of reinforced concrete. Completed six months after his death, it helped cement a reputation that has become the stuff of legend. **PC**

Yakovlev Postnik

Dates: Sixteenth century   **Nationality:** Russian   **Location:** Moscow, Russia   **Date Completed:** 1560   **Style | Movement:** Byzantine / Russian

According to legend, architect Postnik Yakovlev and master mason Ivan Shiryai (nicknamed 'Barma') were blinded by Tsar Ivan IV (the Terrible) after finishing St Basil's, to ensure they could not duplicate it. The story is probably untrue—Postnik and Barma are also said to have gone on to Kazan, where they built the walls of the Kremlin and the Cathedral of the Annunciation. St Basil's, built on the orders of Ivan IV to celebrate the capture of Kazan from the Tatars in 1552 is, however, quite beautiful. The multi-coloured scheme of its eight onion domes was applied in 1860; originally, it was painted white with gold domes. Officially it is named the Cathedral of the Intercession of the Virgin by the Moat; Basil the Blessed, a so-called 'holy fool', who died in 1557, was buried there and gives it its popular name. In the Orthodox Church the eight-pointed star holds great significance and represents, among other things, the Virgin, accounting for the eight domed chapels. There is debate about the influences behind the building style: much can be attributed to Russia's position between Europe and the East, as St Basil's has sympathy with both Muslim architecture and with that of the Byzantine Empire, whose Orthodox faith the Russians shared. **SF**

Yamasaki Minoru

Dates: 1920–86   **Nationality:** American   **Location:** New York, NY, United States   **Date Completed:** 1973 (destroyed 2001)   **Style|Movement:** Modernist

The development of the skyscraper remains America's dominant contribution to the history of architecture, and architect Minoru Yamasaki provides a direct link between two of its tallest examples. A second-generation Japanese-American, Yamasaki studied architecture at New York University before gaining employment with Shreve, Lamb & Harmon in 1937. Expert at skyscraper design, the practice's most prestigious project had been the Empire State Building (1931), which remained the world's tallest building for 40 years. By a quirk of fate, it would be Yamasaki who would strip his former employers of that title, when the north tower of his World Trade Center was topped out in 1971, followed a year later by its identical twin. The bulk of the towers' structure was placed around their perimeters, with a steel tube frame arrangement of 59 columns down each facade. Yamasaki chose to articulate this construction with dense ribbons of silvery aluminium alloy that converged in gothic arches near ground level to admit more light into the double-height atrium. Sadly, it was this forest of glittering metal strips that was to provide the most haunting image of the towers after the horrific attacks of September 11, 2001, when the tangled trees of twisted aluminium were left silhouetted above the dark piles of debris. **PC**

Zimmermann Dominikus

Pilgrimage Church of the Scourged Saviour

Dates: 1685–1766   **Nationality:** German   **Location:** Wies, Bavaria, Germany   **Date Completed:** 1754   **Style | Movement:** Rococo

In 1738, in the small hamlet of Wies in Bavaria, tears were said to appear in the eyes of a wooden statue of Christ at the whipping post. Before too long, pilgrims started to visit and, in 1745, the local abbot asked Dominikus Zimmermann to create a more suitable building for housing the miraculous statue. Zimmermann had started his working life as an altar builder and marbler before learning stucco work. He and his brother Johann Baptist—himself a notable court stuccoist and a fresco painter—had

worked together refurbishing Buxheim Charterhouse, then designing the Dominican convent church at Mödingen (1716–21), and a pilgrimage church in Steinhausen. Called 'the most beautiful village church in the world,' the Steinhausen church is built on an oval pattern with rococo decoration in coloured stucco and painted frescoes and is very similar to Wies. Both were also *Gesamtkunstwerke* (total art works) in which Dominikus and Johann did almost all the work themselves. As with so many

eighteenth-century churches, the plain exterior does not prepare the visitor for the exuberant explosion of colour and art inside. Wies's interior is covered in rich stucco work, the gold standing out brightly from the white. The nave's ceiling, supported by eight pairs of pillars, has a sublime fresco by Baptist. Peter Dörfler called it 'a bit of heaven in this suffering world'. This rococo jewel became a UNESCO World Heritage Site in 1983. **SF**

Zumthor Peter

Dates: Born 1943　**Nationality:** Swiss　**Location:** Vals, Switzerland　**Date Completed:** 1996　**Style|Movement:** Modernist

Based in a remote village high in the Swiss mountains, Peter Zumthor deliberately isolates himself from the transient concerns of modern-day life as he searches for timeless solutions. Supported by a small team of 15 employees, he is dedicated to detailing every last aspect of his work. Each of his exquisite projects is distinguished by the careful selection of materials and finishes with which he choreographs the moods and emotions within his controlled environments. Zumthor's early training in cabinet-making comes through in his attention to detail, and in his writings he describes the simple tactile experience of touching a door handle as a Proustian trigger for past memories. Zumthor spent 10 years surveying and preserving the historic monuments of the Swiss canton of Grisons as a conservation architect, and the sensitivity and care with which he now approaches each project site bears comparison with an archaeological dig. One of his most revered compositions, the Thermal Baths at Vals takes the experience of bathing back to antiquity, reducing it to the simple sensory experience of stone and water. Within this warm, dark cave of locally quarried Valser quarzite slabs, bathers are left to focus on the restorative effects of the pure spring water, in a truly immersive experience. **PC**

Chronology

	Dates	Name	Building	Page number
14th — 15th c.	1377—1446	Brunelleschi, Filippo	The Basilica di Santa Maria del Fiore | Duomo	32
	1404—72	Alberti, Leon Battista	Basilica of Santa Maria Novella	12
	1444—1514	Bramante, Donato	Tempietto San Pietro in Montorio	31
	1475—1564	Buonarroti, Michelangelo	Piazza del Campidoglio	33
	16th century	Yakovlev, Postnik	St. Basil's Cathedral	206
16th century	1508—80	Palladio, Andrea (Andrea di Pietro della Gondola)	Villa Almerico Capra | La Rotonda	141
	1512—72	Alessi, Galeazzo	Church of St. Barnabas and St. Paul	13
	c.1514—70	Delorme, Philibert (also de L'Orme)	Chateau de Chenonceau	51
	c.1540—c. 1617	Mehmed Ağa	Sultan Ahmed Mosque | The Blue Mosque	123
	1573—1652	Jones, Inigo	Queen's House	94
	1598—1680	Bernini, Gian Lorenzo	Colonnades in front of St. Peter's Basilica	25
	1599—1667	Borromini, Francesco	San Carlo alle Quattro Fontane	28
17th century	1632—1723	Wren, Christopher	St. Paul's Cathedral	204
	1646—1708	Hardouin-Mansart, Jules	Third phase of the Palace of Versailles	75
	1650—1719	Talman, William	Chatsworth House | east and south facades	179
	1661—1736	Hawksmoor, Nicholas	St. George's Church	76
	1664—1726	Vanbrugh, John	Blenheim Palace	189
	1678—1736	Juvarra, Filippo	Basilica di Superga	95
	1682—1754	Gibbs, James	Radcliffe Camera	68
	1685—1766	Zimmermann, Dominikus	Pilgrimage Church of the Scourged Saviour	208
	1694—1753	Boyle, Richard	Chiswick House Villa	30
	1698—1782	Gabriel, Ange-Jacques	Chateau of the Petit Trianon	63
	1699—1753	Knobelsdorff, Georg Wenzeslaus von	Schloss Sanssouci	102
	18th century	Ustad, Lal Chand	Hawa Mahal | Palace of the Winds	186
18th century	1700—64	Sacchetti, Giovanni Battista	Palacio Real de Madrid | Royal Palace	160
	1700—71	Rastrelli, Bartolomeo Francesco	Winter Palace	152
	1723—96	Chambers, William	Somerset House	40
	1728—82	Wood the Younger, John	Royal Crescent	203
	1728—92	Adam, Robert	Syon House	11
	1732—1808	Langhans, Carl Gotthard	Brandenburg Gate	108
	1739—1811	Villanueva, Juan de	Museo del Prado | Prado Museum	192
	1743—1826	Jefferson, Thomas	Monticello	90
	1752—1835	Nash, John	Royal Pavilion	132
	1753—1837	Soane, John	Sir John Soane's Museum	173
	1764—1820	Latrobe, Benjamin Henry	The White House	111
	1780—1867	Smirke, Robert	British Museum	172
	1781—1841	Schinkel, Karl Friedrich	Altes Museum	165
	1788—1855	Cubitt, Thomas	Osbourne House	48
	1788—1863	Cockerell, Charles Robert	Interior of St. Georges Hall	45
19th c.	1795—1860	Barry, Charles	Palace of Westminster | Houses of Parliament	21
	1800—81	Burton, Decimus	The Palm House	36

Dates	Name	Building	Page number
1801—75	Labrouste, Pierre-François-Henri	Reading Room of Bibliothèque Sainte Geneviève	107
1803—79	Semper, Gottfried	Semperoper | Opera house	169
1803—92	Davis, Alexander Jackson	Federal Hall National Memorial	50
1804—87	Walter, Thomas Ustick	Capitol Building | wings and cast-iron dome	196
1811—78	Scott, George Gilbert	Midland Grand Hotel	166
1812—52	Pugin, Augustus	St Giles	151
1814—1900	Butterfield, William	Keble College Chapel	37
1823—65	Fowke, Captain Francis	Royal Albert Hall	60
1825—98	Garnier, Jean-Louis Charles	Paris Opéra | Palais Garnier	64
1827—81	Burges, William	Cardiff Castle	34
1829—77	Mengoni, Giuseppe	Galleria Vittorio Emanuele II	127
1830—1905	Waterhouse, Alfred	Natural History Museum	197
1831—1912	Shaw, Richard Norman	New Scotland Yard | Norman Shaw Buildings	170
1831—1915	Webb, Philip	The Red House	199
1832—1923	Eiffel, Alexandre Gustave	Eiffel Tower	55
1841—1918	Wagner, Otto	Karlsplatz Stadtbahn Station	195
1846—1912	Burnham, Daniel Hudson	Flatiron Building	35
1849—1930	Webb, Aston	Victoria and Albert Museum	198
1849—1930	Wilkinson, Chris and Eyre, Jim	Gateshead Millennium Bridge	201
1851—1928	Townsend, Charles Harrison	Horniman Museum	182
1852—1926	Gaudí, Antoni (Antoni Gaudí i Cornet)	La Sagrada Familia	65
1853—1930	Jensen-Klint, Peder Vilhelm	Grundtvigskirken | Grundtvig's Church	91
1856—1924	Sullivan, Louis Henry	Bayard-Condict Building	177
1856—1934	Berlage, Hendrik Petrus	Beurs van Berlage	24
1857—1941	Voysey, Charles F.A.	Annesley Lodge	194
1861—1925	Steiner, Rudolf	Goetheanum	175
1861—1947	Horta, Victor	Maison Horta	85
1863—1940	Unwin, Raymond	Corringham Road	185
1863—1957	Velde, Henry van de	Van de Velde Building	190
1865—1945	Baillie Scott, Mackay Hugh	Blackwell House	19
1866—1945	Östberg, Ragnar	Stockholm Town Hall	137
1867—1908	Olbrich, Joseph	Wiener Secessionsgebäude | The Viennese Secession Building	136
1867—1959	Wright, Frank Lloyd	Solomon R. Guggenheim Museum	205
1868—1928	Mackintosh, Charles Rennie	Hill House	119
1868—1940	Behrens, Peter	AEG Turbine Factory	23
1868—1957 (Charles) 1870—1954 (Henry)	Greene, Charles Sumner and Henry Mather	David Gamble House	71
1869—1944	Lutyens, Edwin	Folly Farm | west wing	118
1870—1933	Loos, Adolf	Villa Müller	116
1870—1956	Hoffmann, Josef Franz Maria	Palais Stoclet	80
1872—1957	Plečnik, Jože	Church of the Sacred Heart	148

Dates	Name	Building	Page number
1873—1950	Saarinen, Eliel	Helsinki Central Railway Station	159
1874—1954	Perret, Auguste	Church of Notre Dame du Raincy	146
1875—1960	Holden, Charles Henry	Arnos Grove	81
1880—1960	Scott, Giles Gilbert	Battersea Power Station	167
1882—1954	Tait, Thomas Smith	Daily Telegraph Offices	178
1883—1950	Chareau, Pierre	Rue St. Guillaume, La Maison de Verre | House of Glass	41
1883—1954	Van Alen, William	Chrysler Building	188
1883—1969	Gropius, Walter	Bauhaus Dessau	73
1884—1923	Klerk, Michel de	Het Schip	101
1884—1974	Dudok, Willem Marinus	Hilversum Town Hall	52
1885—1940	Asplund, Gunnar Erik	Stockholm Public Library	18
1885—56	Rudnev, Lev	Lomonosov Moscow State University	156
1886—1969	Mies van der Rohe, Ludwig	Barcelona Pavilion | a.k.a. German Pavilion	128
1887—1953	Mendelsohn, Erich	Einsteinturm | Einstein Tower	126
1887—1965	Le Corbusier (Charles-Edouard Jeanneret-Gris)	Notre-Dame-du-Haut Chapel	113
1888—1964	Rietveld, Gerrit Thomas	Rietveld Schröder House	153
1890—1974	Melnikov, Konstantin	Melnikov House	125
1891—1979	Ponti, Gio	Montedoria Offices	149
1892—1970	Neutra, Richard	Kaufmann Desert House	133
1893—1972	Scharoun, Hans	Philharmonie | Berlin Philharmonic	164
1895—1958	Coates, Wells	Isokon Building | Lawn Road Flats	44
1895—1983	Fuller, Richard Buckminster	Biosphere	62
1898—1976	Aalto, Alvar	Riola Parish Church | Church of the Assumption of Mary	10
1900—96	Chermayeff, Serge	De La Warr Pavilion	42
1901—74	Kahn, Louis	The National Assembly Building of Bangladesh	97
1901—80	Connell, Amyas	High & Over | The Aeroplane House	46
1901—90	Lubetkin, Berthold	Penguin Pool	117
1902—71	Jacobsen, Arne	St. Catherine's College	88
1902—87	Goldfinger, Ernö	Trellick Tower	69
1902—88	Barragàn, Luis	San Cristobal Stables & Folke Egerstrom House	20
1906—2005	Johnson, Philip	AT&T Building | now Sony Building	93
1906—78	Scarpa, Carlo	Brion-Vega Cemetery	163
1907—2012	Niemeyer, Oscar	National Congress	134
1907—78 (Charles) 1912—88 (Ray)	Eames, Charles and Ray	Eames House | Case Study House No. 8	54
1908—94	Gibberd, Frederick Ernest	Liverpool Metropolitan Cathedral	67
1910—61	Saarinen, Eero	Trans World Airlines | TWA Terminal	158
1911—94	Lautner, John	Chemosphere | Malin Residence	112
1913—2005	Tange, Kenzo	Fuji-Sankei Communications Group Headquarters Building	180
1914—2001	Lasdun, Denys	National Theatre	110
1914—2005	Erskine, Ralph	The Ark	57

19th century

20th century

20th century

Dates	Name	Building	Page number
1937—	Piano, Renzo	Jean-Marie Tjibaou Cultural Center	147
1937—	Terry, Quinlan	Richmond Riverside	181
1937—2009	Kaplický, Jan	Natwest Media Centre	98
1938—	Andreu, Paul	National Centre for the Performing Arts	16
1938—	Farrell, Terry	The Deep	58
1938—	Safdie, Moshe	Habitat 67	161
1938—	Wilford, Michael	The Lowry Centre for the Performing Arts	200
1939—	Grimshaw, Nicholas	Eden Project	72
1939—	Jiřičná, Eva	Joseph Store	92
1940—	Jahn, Helmut	Bahn Tower | Sony Center	89
1941—	Andō, Tadao	Kidosaki House	15
1941—	Ito, Toyo	2002 Serpentine Pavilion	87
1943—	Botta, Mario	Church of San Giovanni Battista	29
1943—	Outram, John	Storm Water Pumping Station	140
1943—	Zumthor, Peter	Thermal Baths	209
1944—	Fuksas, Massimiliano	FieraMilano Complex	61
1944—	Koolhaas, Rem	Seattle Public Library	104
1944—	Mayne, Thom	Caltrans District 7 Headquarters	121
1944—	Tschumi, Bernard	Parc de La Villette	183
1944—	Viñoly, Rafael	International Forum	193
1945—	Nouvel, Jean	Institut du Monde Arabe | IMA	135
1946—	Libeskind, Daniel	Jewish Museum	115
1946—	Ott, Carlos	Opera de la Bastille	138
1947—	Alsop, Will	Peckham Library	14
1947—	Holl, Steven	Het Oosten Pavilion	82
1947—	Prince, Bart	Prince House	150
1948—	Sahba, Fariborz	Bahá'í House of Worship | Lotus Temple	162
1949—	Pawson, John	Neuendorf House	142
1950 (both)—	Herzog, Jacques and de Meuron, Pierre (Herzog & de Meuron)	National Stadium | The Bird's Nest	79
1950—	Hadid, Zaha	Phaeno Science Centre	74
1951—	Arad, Ron	Holon Design Museum	17
1951—	Calatrava, Santiago	City of Arts and Sciences	38
1951—	Kuhne, Eric	Titanic Belfast	105
1953—	Chipperfield, David	Veles e Vents | Americas Cup Pavilion	43
1954—	McAslan, John	King's Cross Station	122
1955—2000	Miralles Moya, Enric	Scottish Parliament	129
1960—	Dunster, Bill	Beddington ZED | BedZED	53
1970—	Heatherwick, Thomas	Seed Cathedral | UK Pavilion	77

20th century

Index

Image Libraries: Arcaid Images, Artur Images, BildarchivMonheim, Corbis Images, Mondadori Electa, Leemage. **Photographers:** Peter Adams (p 162), Bernard Annebicque (p 107), Adrian Alston (p 16), Peter Barritt (p 12), Markus Bassler (p 192), Achim Bednorz (pp 63, 95, 175), Nathan Benn (p 177), John Bower (p 68), Richard Bryant (pp 4, 6 (r), 15, 22, 24, 39, 40, 58, 59, 71, 72, 74, 78, 83, 85, 86, 88, 92, 109, 110, 114, 123, 128, 131, 138, 140, 142, 144, 145, 153, 154, 159, 160, 168, 172, 173, 176, 183, 185, 197, 198, 200), Stefan Buzas (p 163), Demetrio Carrasco (p 156), Julian Castle (pp 136, 195), Paul Cattermole (pp 21, 76), David Churchill (pp 132, 181, 194), David Clapp (pp 45, 152), Neale Clark (p 43), Joe Cornish (p 143), Hufton & Crowe (p 104), Nigel Corrie (p 48), Fridmar Damm (p 157), Cameron Davidson (p 33), Nick Dawe (pp 47, 117), Robert O'Dea (p 36), Colin Dixon (p 170), Yin Dongxun (pp 17, 18), Peter Durant (p 46), Peter Eberts (p 116), Richard Einzig (p 10), Julian Elliott (p 51), Mark Fiennes (pp 119, 148, 158, 191), Tim Franco (p 77), John Gollings (p 147), Roman von Götz (p 11), Tim Griffith (p 79), Fernando Guerra (p 171), Michael Halberstadt (p 41), Michael Harding (pp cover, 62, 66, 161), Chris Heaney (p 105), Jochen Helle (pp 80, 91, 125), John Heseltine (p 31), John Hicks (p 96), Andrew Holbrooke (p 97), Daniel Hopkinson (p 7 (r)), Angelo Hornak (p 182), Werner Huthmacher (p 20), Gavin Jackson (pp 43, 50, 60, 69, 81, 93, 111, 137, 149, 178, 188, 196), Ben Johnson (p 135), Martin Jones (p 189), Nick Kane (pp 44, 82, 98, 129), Rainer Kiedrowski (pp 108, 186), Martine Hamilton Knight (p 84), Lucinda Lambton (pp 35, 151), John Edward Linden (pp 8 (r), 65, 89, 103, 115, 121, 124, 130, 174, 193), Benedict Luxmoore (pp 49, 53, 122), Pol M.R. Maeyaert (p 75), Marcel Malherbe (pp 34, 187), HansPeter Merten (p 169), Florian Monheim (pp 23, 102, 164, 190), Barbara Opitz (p 179), Timothy Pike (p 38), Will Pryce (pp 32, 37, 52, 90, 101, 118, 120, 166, 167), Louie Psihoyos (p 70), Beppe Raso (p 61), Patrick Robert (p 100), Schtüze + Rodemann (pp 27, 29, 73, 139, 141, 184), Fritz von der Schulenburg (p 30), Sylvain Sonnet (p 64), Tino Soriano (p 8(l)), Natalie Tepper (pp 6 (l), 26), Bill Tingey (pp 106, 180), Richard Turpin (p 94), Francesco Venturi (p 28), Richard Waite (pp 14, 87), Jonathan CK Webb (p 67), Alan Weintraub (pp 7(l), 99, 112, 133, 134, 150), Arnd Wiegmann (p 126), Charlotte Wood (pp 18, 199). **Foundations / Collecting Societies:** Luis Barragán: Barragan Foundation, Birsfelden, Switzerland / ProLitteris / DACS, London, Le Corbusier: FLC/ ADAGP, Paris / DACS, London, Jean Nouvel: ADAGP, Paris / DACS, London, Frank Lloyd Wright: ARS, NY / DACS, London.